the barbecue book

the barbecue book

200 recipes, from burgers to banquets

Jim "Mr Barbecue" Marks

EBURY
PRESS

For Brenda, William, Duncan and Helen

1 3 5 7 9 10 8 6 4 2

This new and revised edition published in 2007 by Ebury Publishing
First Published in Great Britain by Kitbridge Publishing Ltd in 2001

Ebury Publishing is a division of the Random House Group

Copyright © Jim Marks 2001, 2007
Photography © Ebury Press 2007, except pages 2, 5, 6 and 8-9 © istockphoto Inc. 2007

Jim Marks has asserted his right to be identified as the author of this Work
in accordance with the Copyright, Designs and Patents Act 1988

The Random House Group Limited Reg. No. 954009

Addresses for companies within the Random House Group can be found at www.randomhouse.co.uk

A CIP catalogue record for this book is available from the British Library

The Random House Group Limited makes every effort to ensure that the papers used in our
books are made from trees that have been legally sourced from well-managed and credibly
certified forests. Our paper procurement policy can be found on www.randomhouse.co.uk

Photographer: Myles New
Design: threedotsperinch.com
Food stylist: Marina Filippelli
Props stylist: Victoria Allen

Printed and bound in Singapore by Tien Wah Press

ISBN 9780091919153

Contents

Foreword

In the comparatively short time I have known Jim Marks, I have learnt two major facts. The first is that Jim can talk like nobody else that I know, and secondly that when I want to know anything about the art of barbecuing, then he's the man.

I live my life cooking and talking about food and drink, and this has always been the love of my life. Now I've discovered barbecuing and fallen in love again – with the art and not Jim, I hasten to add.

So suddenly life is great and all I need to know is here in this book; it's wonderful, aren't I lucky? Wherever you sit on the 'Richter' scale of barbecuing, this book is for you – enjoy.

Brian J. Turner, CBE
Chef/Restaurateur

Introduction

Who knows when, where and by whom, the first piece of meat was cooked over hot coals, but like most great discoveries it probably came about from a happy combination of accident and chance. Tracing outdoor, or 'in cave' cooking, to its prehistoric roots is impossible but archaeologists have unearthed ample evidence that man has been perfecting his open-fire cooking techniques for thousands of years. As far as pictorial evidence of early forms of barbecues is concerned, the famous Bayeux Tapestry depicts a farewell party, held by Odo, Bishop of Bayeux, in honour of his liege lord William Duke of Normandy, just prior to William and his army setting off across the Channel in 1066. The relevant panels show busy servants offering the guests a generous selection of kebabs, sausages and spit-roast chickens, all cooked, it would appear, on the French equivalent of open barbecues. Despite my misgivings, I must support the hypothesis that this hearty consumption of barbecue fare by William and his men had a direct, some might say unfair, bearing on the outcome of William's forthcoming engagement at Hastings.

The modern barbecue phenomenon probably took root in the British colony of Virginia in the latter part of the seventeenth century, when the settlers embarked on the practice of holding large social gatherings centred on outdoor cooking feasts. As far as the word 'barbecue' itself is concerned, my vote goes to the theory that it is a bastard form of *barbe à queue* ('whiskers to tail'), a phrase reputedly used by French settlers in Louisiana to characterize spit-roasting a whole animal.

For me there is no mystery as to why barbecuing has developed into such a hugely popular worldwide pastime. It is the almost magical combination of fire, food, family, friends and fun that does the trick. What other social pursuit produces so much pleasure, with so little effort and cost?

As you will, hopefully, deduce from the recipes on the following pages, one can tackle virtually any type of food on a barbecue and cater for most tastes and occasions, be it breakfast, lunch, a sophisticated dinner or large-scale party. I have enjoyed barbecuing on the beach (see page 166), on balconies, on board boats, in car parks, in TV studios, on the river bank and on patios. For a growing number of aficionados, barbecue time is any time and, if the weather is somewhat inclement one can, with a covered barbecue, cook out and eat in. So anyone owning a lidded barbecue who doesn't press it into service on Christmas Day, regardless of snow or rain, is wasting a golden opportunity to conjure up a truly magnificent turkey, perhaps a joint of beef, whilst at the same time liberating stacks of valuable oven space.

Happy barbecuing!

Jim Marks

Getting Started

Choosing a barbecue

Such is the huge range and diversity of barbecue equipment currently available, one can appreciate why coming to a decision as to which to purchase can prove a little difficult.

Bearing in mind that some barbecues can be similar in price to major household appliances, such as dishwashers and refrigerators, it makes sense to carry out some basic research before setting out for the barbecue emporium. You need to consider the following:

- Does gas, charcoal or wood-burning best serve your needs?
- What size do you need?
- Can it handle the normal demands that will be placed on it?
- What cooking techniques do you wish to pursue?

If, for example, you would like to roast and smoke-cook meats, or bake bread, pies, etc., then you will require a barbecue with a lid. If, on the other hand, your culinary ambitions stop short at grilling fast-cooking foods such as burgers, cutlets, chicken portions and fish, then barbecues such as the braziers and flat tops will fully fit the bill. Set yourself a budget to work to, which should include, if you are starting out from scratch, such items as tools and accessories and of course fuel and firelighters.

For advice on the different types of barbecues available, as well as tools and accessories, see the Guide to Equipment on pages 166–80.

Fuel

Leaving gas-burning barbecues to one side, experienced practitioners of the art will tell you that the success, or otherwise, of all cookouts hinges on the quality of the fuel being used. Charcoal can vary enormously in this respect, so before blaming yourself or your equipment for an unsatisfactory performance, you might want to consider whether the charcoal itself was up to scratch. It should be:

- relatively easy to get started;
- capable of providing an excellent level of heat;
- long-burning.

If in doubt, try another brand and, if necessary, keep doing so until you find one that meets these requirements.

Lumpwood charcoal

This is charcoal that comes straight from the kiln in lumps of varying sizes, which are then broken up into graded pieces deemed suitable for barbecuing. Good-quality lumpwood charcoal should be bone-dry and feel light for its bulk. There should be minimal dust in the bottom of the bag. The best-quality lumpwood charcoal is made from hardwoods (beech, etc.) but it is not uncommon for some softwoods to find their way into the kiln. It takes roughly 6 tons of green wood (and a lot of skill) to make just 1 ton of charcoal. Lumpwood charcoal's main advantage is that it is relatively easy to light.

Charcoal briquettes

All briquettes are made from pulverised materials – be it 100% hardwood char, a mixture of hardwood char and mineral carbons, or (in the case of one very popular

Getting Started

Australian brand) the product is made from mineral carbon which burns hotter and longer. A starch, or similar, compound is used to bind the pulverised material into pillow-shaped briquettes. Briquettes burn for about twice as long as lumpwood charcoal, which makes them particularly suitable for tackling long-cooking large roasts. Due to their dense composition, briquettes can sometimes prove difficult to ignite. Instant-lighting charcoal, which is now universally available, can be ready for use some 20 minutes after the paper bag it is packed in, is lit.

N.B. Never add this form of charcoal to an established fire as the fumes given off in the early stages will adulterate any food on the grill.

Wood

Virtually any hardwood, providing it is well-seasoned, can be used, with beech probably being the most readily available followed by oak, birch, ash, apple and cherry. Vine cuttings are easy to light, but you will require a goodly amount to produce sufficient cooking heat, for even a relatively short time, which tends to limit its use to fast-cooking food such as small fish, cutlets, chicken wings, etc.

Firelighters

 WARNING: Never use petrol, methylated spirits, lighter fluid, kerosene, naptha or similar volatile liquids to light your fire. **IT IS DANGEROUS BOTH FOR YOU AND THOSE STANDING NEARBY!** Never add more starter fluid to a charcoal or wood fire that has already been ignited, even if it does not appear to be burning. Should you wish to rekindle the fire, use a solid firelighter. If in any doubt, it is safer to start the fire again from scratch.

Solid firelighters

Widely used for many years to start the home fires burning, the familiar solid white block has become equally popular with the barbecue fraternity. Unfortunately, when it has been lit, this traditional firelighter emits a rather unpleasant odour combined with a certain amount of black smoke. However, both the smoke and the odour will have dissipated well before the fire is ready to cook on. A 'smokeless' version of the solid firelighter is, however, available which is non-toxic, odourless and clean burning.

Liquid firelighter

Commercial liquid firelighters specifically sold for barbecue use are non-volatile, but nevertheless should not be added to a lit fire.

Jellied alcohol (lighter paste)

Somewhat expensive for home-based barbecues, but a very convenient starter for picnic ones.

Blow torch

Good results can be achieved with a compact blow torch as used for DIY jobs around the house, and by chefs for putting the finishing touches to crème brûlée, but it does require the user to be on hand for a few minutes until the fire takes hold.

Charcoal chimney

A charcoal chimney comprises a metal tube, handle attached, roughly 15cm (6 inches) in diameter and 30cm (12 inches) long. The chimney is placed on the barbecue's grate, and two or three crumpled sheets of newspaper are stuffed into the bottom of the tube, plus perhaps a few small pieces of kindling. The chimney is then filled with charcoal and the paper is lit. Once the charcoal has ignited – this should take only 15 minutes or so – carefully remove the chimney and spread out the coals as required.

Cooking Techniques

In this introduction to cooking techniques, I've divided the advice into two segments according to whether you're using a charcoal or wood-burning barbecue, or a gas one. Just follow whatever's appropriate for your needs.

Open grill cooking

Open grill cooking, direct cooking or just plain grilling all mean the same thing: cooking food directly over radiant heat, from whatever its source. Grilling is the most popular and widely practised of all the barbecue cooking techniques and for many people, it is synonymous with 'barbecuing' – hardly surprising, bearing in mind that the word and the activity have been so closely related for centuries.

Grilling requires the cook's constant attention, so anything that can be cooked in 30 minutes or less is a suitable candidate for this method, e.g. steaks, chops, chicken and turkey portions, hamburgers, sausages, kebabs, whole fish and fish steaks. One exception would be Butterflied leg of lamb in a herb crust (see page 96) where the grilling time could be between 40 and 50 minutes, depending on the weight and thickness of the joint.

I've provided a broad guide to grilling times on page 182, but always bear in mind that air temperature and wind strength can have a marked effect on the cooking times quoted. However, for those owners of

covered barbecues intent on barbecuing some steaks, regardless of how awful the weather is, all they have to do is to carry on cooking with the lid in position. A considerable volume of smoke will be produced, but as much of it will be trapped under the lid, this will only add an additional je ne sais quoi to the steaks' appearance and flavour!

Grilling

On charcoal-burning barbecues
1. Start your fire, following the instructions set out on page 173. Wait until most of the charcoal is covered in grey ash before starting to cook.
2. Prior to placing the grill on the barbecue, brush the grill bars with vegetable oil to lubricate them, or perhaps rub with some of the fat that has been trimmed from the meat. Also grease the griddle plate if your barbecue incorporates one and you are planning to use it.
3. If your barbecue has an adjustable height grill, adjust the level of the grill to about 8cm (3–4 inches) above the fire-bed. Cooking at this level for a minute or so will sear the surface of the meat, thereby locking in those valuable juices which make such a valuable contribution to the meat's succulence.

On gas barbecues
1. Remove the food grill(s) before lighting the gas and brush over with cooking oil to lubricate. If some fat has been trimmed from the meat, you could use this as a natural lubricant. Also grease the griddle plate if your barbecue incorporates one and you are planning to use it.
2. With the lid open, ignite the gas burners at the high heat setting. Close the lid and allow the barbecue's fire-bed (volcanic rock, etc.) to reach grilling heat – this should take 5–10 minutes depending on the state of the weather and the barbecue model.
3. Replace the food grill(s) just prior to the commencement of cooking.
4. Adjust the gas control knobs to the required setting (more on this follows).
5. Position the food on the grill(s). Avoid crowding

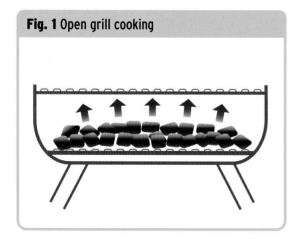

Fig. 1 Open grill cooking

Cooking Techniques

the grill surface, especially with fatty foods such as sausages, hamburgers, chicken pieces, etc.

6. As a general rule, select a low to medium heat setting when tackling fish, vegetables and fruit and a medium heat for beef, pork, lamb and poultry. Aside from pre-heating and helping to clean the barbecue, the high heat setting may be used occasionally for searing steaks, etc., but culinarily speaking, for very little else.

Top grilling tips:

- If you are using a thick basting sauce – containing sugar, jam, honey or ketchup – brush it on during the final few minutes of cooking. If applied too early, especially at high cooking temperatures, the surface of the meat will quickly burn and char.
- Grill one side of the meat for the time recommended in the recipe or cooking time chart. Brush the uncooked surface with oil or butter. Turn the meat over and complete the cooking cycle.
- Marinating meat for a few hours or overnight in the refrigerator moistens, flavours and tenderises it. A cheaper lean cut, such as chuck, will benefit from an oil-based marinade.
- Use long-handled tongs, with 'soft jaws', to turn steaks. Tongs that have sharp teeth may pierce the meat and accidentally cause the loss of precious juices.
- Thaw frozen meat while it marinates. Simply keep the meat in the marinade, turning it a few times if it is not completely immersed.

Grilling Kebabs

For sheer versatility, skewer-cooking takes some beating! It alone gives the cook a completely free rein to produce a boundless variety of food with which to please the palates of all and sundry. Meat, poultry, fish, vegetables and fruit can all be cooked on a skewer, separately or in colourful, mouth-watering combinations. If necessary, the taste and tenderness of the kebabs can be further enhanced by marinating the food with wine, herbs and spices.

Top kebab tips:

- Oiling metal skewers prior to threading on chunks of meat and fish will help to prevent the food from sticking. Bamboo skewers, traditionally used for satay, should be soaked in water before use in order to reduce the chances of their burning during cooking.
- When cutting up chunks of fish for impaling on a skewer, leaving on the skin of the fish will help to hold the flesh together while it is being pierced and, later, while it is being cooked.
- Matching the contents of a skewer with food of a roughly similar cooking span will help to produce balanced results. Alternatively, part-cooking the slower-cooking food prior to making up the complete skewer will help to even out the disparity, e.g. for mixed vegetable kebabs, parboiling the harder, slower-cooking items, such as corn on the cob, small onions and potatoes, will help to even out cooking times.
- Use the warming grill (rack) of your barbecue to support and gently cook all-vegetable kebabs whilst in the process of cooking meat on the grill below. Finishing off the vegetables on the main grill will give them some attractive sear marks to match those of the meat.
- Trim excess fat from meat to help reduce potential flare-ups (see page 174 for some helpful hints on how to avoid these).
- Finally, try not to 'log jam' the skewer with food – particularly meat. Leave small gaps so that the heat can get through to all surfaces.

'Indirect heat' cooking

It is entirely possible and very practical – particularly when the weather is inclement – to use a covered barbecue for fast-cooking food such as steaks, chops and hamburgers, but to extract the maximum benefit from your investment in a covered unit, it should be regularly pressed into service to roast joints, whole birds and thick slabs of meat. If it isn't, it could be regarded as tantamount to driving your dream sports car half a mile to the village post office – once a week! You should give

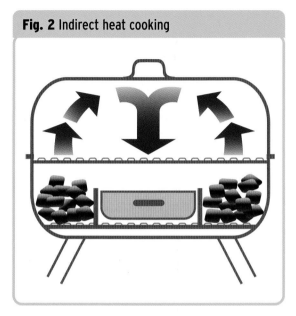

Fig. 2 Indirect heat cooking

serious consideration to treating your covered barbecue as a trusted deputy to its kitchen-bound sidekick, and employ it at every opportunity throughout the spring and summer. One has to bear in mind that, aside from turning out superb roasts, a covered barbecue can be used to bake anything from bread to apple pies (more on this, below).

Summertime is obviously the peak barbecue period, but I would argue that Christmas Day offers a golden opportunity to drag your mothballed barbecue from the back of the garage, in order to relieve the considerable pressure the day brings on the kitchen oven (not to mention the hard-pressed cook and washing-up brigade). For more, on this charitable opportunity, see page 65.

Roasting

On charcoal-burning barbecues
Start the fire, following the instructions on page 174. Place the joint on the grill directly over the pan. With the lid in position, the heat from the

fire-bed will reflect off the lid to roast the joint just like your kitchen oven does.

On gas barbecues
Place a drip pan under the grill, to one side of the barbecue for two burner units or in the centre of the grill for 3–4 burner units. Ideally the pan should be large enough to catch all the fats falling away from the food set on the grill above, but not so large that its bulk intrudes into the barbecue's lit-burner area. With the lid in the open position, ignite the gas burner, using the high heat setting, adjacent to (not under) where the drip pan is sitting.

Close the lid and leave the barbecue for 5–10 minutes. Having placed the food on the grill immediately above the drip pan, re-close the lid.

Adjust the temperature setting as required (the 'Medium' heat setting should be adequate for most dishes). If intending to place the food on the barbecue immediately upon ignition, do remember to adjust the heat setting to the required level as soon as the warm-up period has been completed.

Baking

Imagine: a magnificent roast chicken has just been removed from the barbecue to rest and allow its juices to settle down, before it is carved and served to the hungry horde. Waiting quietly in the wings to take its place, is an unbaked apple pie or, better still, a bread and butter pudding. By now, the heat from the fire-bed is likely to be in an ideal state to bake the pie or the pudding so, having placed the dessert in the spot previously occupied by the chicken, the lid is replaced and the barbecue left to carry on baking. Some 30 or 40 minutes later, the lid of the barbecue is removed to reveal a truly scrumptious dish which, although 'barbecue-baked', will certainly not have inherited a barbecue flavour! Bread that has been baked under the lid of a covered barbecue always looks and tastes great. A pizza, hot and bubbling off the barbecue, is a fairly close match (visually, at least) to one that has been prepared in a wood-fired oven.

Cooking Techniques

Baking procedure

If planning to bake something from scratch, simply follow the roasting directions set out on page 15. You may, if you wish to, omit the drip pan, with the proviso that doing so does not allow the charcoal fire-bed to inch its way towards the centre of the grate.

Smoke-cooking

On charcoal or gas barbecues

Do not confuse 'smoke-cooking' with 'smoking' (smoke-curing). Smoking is a slow, highly skilled process, the primary aim being to preserve the meat and fish. This will require a working temperature as low as 10°C (50°F) and can take

Fig. 3 Smoke-cooking

several days to complete. Smoke-cooking, on the other hand, is a 'hot' process, carried out at normal oven temperatures, the exception being the smoker barbecues (see below), which operate in the 80–100°C (175–210°F) range. Whilst contributing very little to the food, preservation-wise, smoke-cooking undoubtedly helps to give meat and poultry a richer, deeper colour and a more piquant flavour than food that has been roasted in the normal manner.

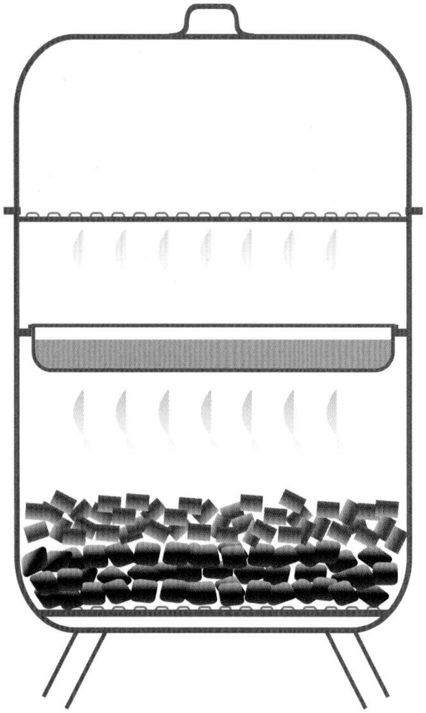

One can 'smoke-cook' food in any charcoal or gas-fired covered barbecue – the cooking times being similar to regular barbecuing. As well as ham, poultry, pork (including spare ribs), lamb, venison, kidneys and sausages, a wide variety of fish and shellfish – such as trout, mackerel, salmon, eel and oysters – are all excellent fare for this highly satisfying barbecue cooking technique.

On smoker barbecues

The smoking of food in a smoker barbecue (often referred to as a water smoker) could be described as a halfway house between the traditional, ultra-slow and highly skilled smoke-curing process at low temperatures, and 'hot' smoking at high temperatures. Cooking in a water smoker differs from the latter in two important respects. First, the barbecue performs at temperatures hovering in the 80–100°C (175–210°F) range for lengthy periods (a full pan of charcoal should normally burn for 5–6 hours or even longer). Second, because the meat is slowly cooked (or bathed) in an atmosphere of warm, moist air and aromatic smoke, it retains its natural moisture while becoming infused with a sweet, smoky flavour (see below). Meat cooked in this way is renowned for its succulence and I will never forget the sublime taste and tenderness of a man-sized piece of brisket that had been hickory-smoked overnight, which I lunched on at a renowned barbecue shack in Houston a few years ago.

Smoking woods

Thirty years or so ago, I took my first crack at smoke-cooking. A red 57-cm (22-inch) Weber charcoal kettle barbecue was the modus operandi and a 7 kg (16 lb) turkey the 'sacrificial lamb' (since that time I have put the lid over, and hickory smoke-cooked, several hundred birds of similar weight at my barbecue demonstrations). (See page 65 for how to smoke-cook your Christmas turkey.) In those early days hickory was, generally speaking, the only smoking wood around. Nowadays a wide variety, in chunk, chip or pellet form, is readily available from barbecue stockists.

As with wine, every wood has its own unique characteristic. It is up to you to decide what wood marries best with what food, but the following notes should prove helpful in that respect.

Oak: Imparts a fairly medium flavour. Good with beef, pork and poultry.
Hickory: Still in pole position popularity-wise. Imparts a strong, very distinctive, flavour. Good with all meat.
Apple: Slightly fruity overtones. Best with poultry and pork (particularly ribs).
Mesquite: Strong distinctive flavour. Best used in moderation. Fine with poultry, pork and fish but particularly good with beef.
Cherry: A fairly subtle fruity flavour. Good with poultry, beef and pork.
Alder: One of the weakest smoking woods. A slightly sweet flavour that works well with pork and poultry, but is particularly good for smoking salmon and fish in general.
Pecan: More subtle than hickory. Imparts a sweet nutty flavour. Very good with beef, pork (especially ribs), and poultry.

Never use pine, spruce, cypress, elm, eucalyptus, or indeed any evergreen resinous wood for smoking food. These woods impart a very unpleasant taste to the food, thus harming your standing as a multi-talented barbecue cook!

Top smoke-cooking tips:

- If you have a penchant for 'smoky-barbecue'-flavoured baked beans, try putting some canned baked beans into an open pot (I use an old Spanish earthenware pot) and leaving them alongside the meat during the last 20 minutes or so of smoke-cooking a chicken. Stir the beans occasionally to prevent the top layer from drying out and crusting up too much.
- Brushing a glaze over the surface of a smoke-cooked joint will add a lovely sheen to the joint's exterior. Do not brush on the glaze too early or it will caramelise and burn – 10–15 minutes before the end of cooking should be fine but do keep an eye on the food.
- Small wood chips tend to burn away quite quickly. 'Bundle-wrapping' (see 'Vegetables in foil', page 20) the water-soaked chips in a couple of layers of foil will help to extend their smoking life. Having made a series of small holes in the package to allow the resultant smoke to escape, place the package on the food grill or directly onto the fire-bed.

Spit-roasting

Watching a leg of lamb, loin of pork, chicken or turkey slowly revolving on a spit, whilst relaxing in your garden chair, quaffing a glass of wine or beer is peculiarly satisfying – indeed, for some it is the culinary equivalent of watching men digging a hole in the road. Small wonder then, that certain catering establishments and in-store delicatessens use a multiple spit-roaster as a powerful magnet with which to attract the punter's attention.

On charcoal-burning barbecues
Apart from small portable units, the majority of charcoal barbecues, be they wagon or brazier models, will allow the user to install a spit-roast assembly (for more information on rotisseries, see page 172).

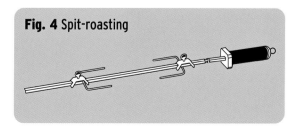

Fig. 4 Spit-roasting

Cooking Techniques

The procedure

Prepare the fire-bed for spit-roasting (see page 174). Having made sure that the prongs on the lower fork are facing away from the handle, pass the spit rod through the centre of the food. In order for the roast to rotate smoothly, it must be evenly balanced on the spit rod. A poorly balanced joint, or bird, will rotate in fits and starts. As a result, there will be excessive wear on the spit motor.

To check that the food on the spit is evenly balanced, rotate the laden spit slowly across the palm of your hands. Should there be little or no tendency for food to roll suddenly from any position, the balance will be good. In the case of a jerky roll, re-skewer the food to correct the imbalance. With a little practice, you should be able to pass the spit rod through the centre of the food's mass regardless of its shape.

When preparing a leg of lamb or leg of pork for spit-roasting, insert the spit into the leg at the fillet end (next to the knuckle of the leg bone). Having carefully pushed the spit through the leg to run alongside the bone, push one of the prongs from the second fork, into the narrow shank end of the leg. If spit-roasting a rib roast, shoulder, or loin, of pork, beef or lamb, insert the spit near the bones at one corner of the joint and push diagonally through the meat until it emerges close to the opposite corner. If spit-roasting poultry or game birds, very carefully push the tip of the spit through the 'parson's nose', into the body cavity and out through the flap of skin at the bird's neck. Having firmly secured the forks, use string to tie the bird into a compact shape.

Try to obtain a steel pan that is narrow in width and fairly shallow in depth. Fill about three-quarters of the drip pan with water or, if you intend using the fat-enriched liquid as a savoury baste, with beer or wine to which a few herbs can be added if you wish.

Position the food-laden spit, and adjust the spit motor so that the food rotates up and away from you. The fats and juices should fall directly into the drip pan – if not, adjust the pan's position accordingly.

On a gas barbecue

A spit-roast assembly (rotisserie) can be fitted to most wagon gas barbecues – a few models have them as a standard accessory and one or two come with a rotisserie burner which, unusually, is fitted at the rear of its lower housing. The largest gas wagons have correspondingly deep lids and burner housings that enable them, with the lid closed, to accommodate a spitted turkey or joint weighing in the region of 9kg (20 lb). Although not a technique that will excite avid 'spit watchers' (referred to above), spit-roasting with the lid down is a lot more energy efficient than spit-roasting carried out on an open barbecue.

The procedure

Remove the food grills and place a steel drip pan (an aluminium pan can be used if your barbecue has a rear-mounted burner) directly on the fire-bed, parallel to, and slightly in front of, where the spit will sit. As mentioned above, try to obtain a pan that is narrow in width and fairly shallow in depth – especially if there is relatively little space between the top of the fire-bed and the spit rod. Again, fill about three-quarters of the pan with water or with a cocktail of water and beer or wine.

With the lid open, ignite the burners at the high heat setting. Close the lid and leave for 5–10 minutes.

Having adjusted the temperature setting (I suggest somewhere in the region of low to medium), place the food-laden spit in position and adjust the spit motor so that the food rotates up and away from you. You may have to slightly adjust the location of the pan to ensure that the fats fall directly into it.

Top spit-roasting tips:
- Unless previously marinated, brush the food with oil at the outset of cooking. Periodically baste joints with some of the liquid from the drip pan.
- If impaling more than one piece of meat on the spit, leave a little space between the pieces to allow the heat to reach all surfaces.
- Periodically, check the level of liquid in the drip pan. It will require topping up now and then, but never pour water into a drip pan where all, or almost all, the liquid has evaporated.

- If you can obtain a rack of spare ribs from your butcher, try spit-roasting them, or failing that, grilling them. Whilst individual ribs might get tucked into a little sooner, the meat in a rib from a rack is a little more succulent, and there is more of it to get your teeth into. Prior to threading the ribs, concertina fashion, onto the spit, trim off any excess fat and strip off any membrane. Having cooked the ribs, basting occasionally with a sauce of your choice (see pages 160–2), it is very easy to slice the rack into individual ribs.

Wok-cooking

Cooking with a wok on your barbecue is a fast, healthy and fun way to prepare a wide array of food at a modest cost. It will, I promise, give you great cachet with family and friends.

This round-bottomed frying pan (wok is the Cantonese word for pan) has been the keystone of the Chinese kitchen for the past 5000 years or so. The wok has no peer when it comes to cooking versatility. Whilst most people are familiar with stir-frying relatively few are aware that the wok is equally adept at steaming, braising, deep-frying and shallow-frying.

It is quite likely that you already own a wok. If so, check to see whether your barbecue will permit the wok to be seated directly on, or very close to, the unit's fire-bed. Unfortunately the shape and size of many charcoal-burning barbecues precludes them from accepting a standard-size domestic wok of about 36cm (14 inches) in diameter. Kettles and open-top brazier charcoal barbecues are the best bet, and the largest models in this category will probably accommodate a larger wok (the larger the wok the better).

Advice on preparing a charcoal fire-bed for wok-cooking is set out on page 173.

Wok-cooking on a gas barbecue

Gas barbecues, particularly those models that have side burners, are eminently suitable for wok-cooking.

Fig. 5 Wok-cooking

In stir-frying what is needed is speed of cooking and, consequently instant heat, i.e. the ability to turn the heat instantly up when required, as well as instantly down. In this particular respect, a gas barbecue has the edge on a charcoal-burning barbecue.

As a rule, the larger the barbecue and the greater its BTU/kilowatt rating, the better.

The procedure

If your gas barbecue has a side burner, ignite the burner at full heat and place the wok squarely on the burner's trivet. Should the wok be one-handled, with a round bottom, a trivet stand will help to keep it stable during cooking. Adjust the burner control knob to the required setting.

If your gas barbecue does not have a side burner, start by removing the food grills. Ignite the burners at the high heat setting, close the lid (if it is a covered unit) and leave for 5–10 minutes. Position the wok on the fire-bed, adjust the burners to the required heat and start cooking.

Top wok-cooking tips:

- Removing the fire-bed (layer of volcanic rock or ceramic briquettes) from your gas barbecue before ignition will allow the wok's bottom to be that little bit closer to the burners, thus effectively increasing the wok's work rate.

Cooking Techniques

- Wrapping two or three layers of foil around the bottom of the wok's handle will help to prevent the wood being scorched by the heat rising from the burners.

Top stir-frying tips:
- Always heat the wok over high heat for a minute or so before adding the oil.
- Prior to placing any food in the wok, turn the wok so that its surface is coated with oil. Dry patches on the surface could result in food sticking, and then burning.
- Make sure your ingredients are completely dry before adding them to the hot oil. When placed in hot oil, food with excess moisture could cause the oil to splatter.
- Cook the recipe ingredients in the recommended order, i.e. spring onions, garlic and ginger should be done first. Vegetables and meat should be cooked separately with the hardest vegetables, such as carrot and celery, being tackled before softer items, such as peppers, with bean sprouts and mushrooms last into the wok.
- Unless the recipe indicates otherwise, use high heat when stir-frying and always turn the contents of the wok from the bottom upwards.
- Before cooking shellfish, place a small chunk of fresh root ginger in the hot oil, and leave for 30 seconds or so. This should slightly mask the fishy aroma and enhance the flavour.
- When you have finished cooking, with the burner still lit add some hot water to the wok and rub over with a mildly abrasive scouring pad until the wok is clean. Having poured out the water, wipe over with a clean cloth and finish drying off over the heat.

Vegetables in foil

The majority of vegetables take very kindly to being grilled on a barbecue over moderate heat, as indeed they undoubtedly do when stir-fried. A healthy alternative, although the results are somewhat bland, is to 'bundle-wrap' them – wrap portions of prepared vegetables in foil and 'steam-cook' them. Cooking vegetables in this manner has its benefits:
- the vegetables retain more of their natural colour, flavour and vitamins than when pot-boiled;
- there is no cleaning of pots and pans.

The procedure
Use heavy-duty (extra thick) foil for wrapping the vegetables. If only thin foil is available, use two or three layers.

I suggest that packs are limited in size so that they can be more easily tucked in around a joint that is being cooked by the 'Indirect heat' method. Two to three average portions can be wrapped in a piece of foil roughly 30 cm (12 inches) square. Having cleaned and prepared the vegetables (leave them wet), place them in the centre of the foil. Lift the four edges of the foil and add some water – 1–2 tablespoons should be sufficient. If you prefer, add a knob of butter (plain or flavoured) in lieu of water.

The wrapping method you employ depends on the cooking technique you intend following.

If using indirect heat, I suggest you 'bundle-wrap' the vegetables. This will require bringing the four corners of the foil square together after you have added the water, to form a rough pyramid shape. Carefully fold the open edges together trying not to crush the package. Keep the package in the upright position.

If it is your intention to cook the vegetables over direct heat, this entails making the package as leak-proof as possible, bearing in mind that it will be turned over fairly frequently. This will therefore require the vegetables to be 'drugstore wrapped'. This entails placing the vegetables in the centre of a square or oblong piece of heavy-duty foil, or two or three layers of thin foil. Having added water, bring the two opposite sides together and turn down the edges in a couple of tight folds ensuring that adequate space is left above the vegetables to allow for heat expansion. Sealing the open ends of the package with a further couple of tight folds will give you a neat, watertight package.

Marinating fish and meat in oil and herbs before barbecuing makes all the difference to the taste and texture of the food (**Spicy lime sardines,** see page 40)

appetisers

Grilled asparagus wrapped in prosciutto; Popcorn; Grilled halloumi with lemon & garlic vinaigrette; Grilled stuffed mushrooms; Bruschetta; Crispy-griddled aubergine wedges; Spicy cheesy potato slices; Olive bacon titbits; Grilled prawns piquant; Prawns with a hint of mint & garlic; Scallop & mushroom teriyaki; Wing drumsticks teriyaki; Barbecued beef morsels.

Grilled asparagus wrapped in prosciutto

Popcorn

Asparagus is an elegant vegetable that will add a touch of savoir faire to your barbecue menu.

Serves 4
12 asparagus spears
2 tablespoons olive oil
6 paper-thin slices of prosciutto, halved lengthways
salt and freshly ground black pepper

Prepare the barbecue for grilling, following the instructions on **page 12**.

Snap the hard end off each asparagus spear and place in a shallow dish. Generously drizzle with the olive oil, sprinkle on some salt and pepper and toss to coat.

Place the asparagus spears on the grill and cook for about 15 minutes, turning halfway through, until the asparagus is tender.

Allow the spears to cool completely before neatly wrapping each one with a piece of prosciutto, leaving the tip exposed.

Arrange on a platter and serve.

3 tablespoons popping corn
1 tablespoon vegetable oil
1 tablespoon golden syrup
(optional)

Prepare the barbecue for grilling, following the instructions on **page 12**.

Place the popping corn and oil in the centre of a double thickness of foil. Bundle-wrap (see 'Vegetables in foil', page 20) leaving plenty of room for the corn to pop around and expand. Place the package over a hot grill and shake occasionally using long-handled tongs. When the popping has ceased, pour the popcorn into a bowl and mix in the golden syrup, if using.

Grilled halloumi with lemon & garlic vinaigrette

Serves 4

This makes a very tasty appetiser with great visual appeal. Halloumi (which originates in Cyprus) is sold in block form. It is stored in its own brine, in sealed packs, and will keep for 5–6 days in a refrigerator after the pack is opened, providing it remains in its brine. In order to bring an extra ray of Mediterranean sunshine to the vinaigrette, lemon juice has been substituted for the more usual wine vinegar.

1 halloumi cheese

For the lemon and garlic vinaigrette:
1 tablespoon lemon juice
1 garlic clove, very finely chopped
1 teaspoon freshly ground black pepper
1 rounded teaspoon mustard powder
1 tablespoon chopped fresh coriander leaves
3 tablespoons extra virgin olive oil

Prepare the barbecue for grilling, following the instructions on **page 12**.

Unwrap the cheese, rinse under cold running water and pat dry with kitchen paper. Cut the block into 8 even slices.

Place the vinaigrette ingredients in a small bowl and whisk together until thoroughly blended. If making the vinaigrette in advance, store it in a screw-top jar and shake vigorously prior to using.

Place the cheese slices on the grill and cook over medium-high heat for about 1 minute on each side or until the halloumi is a light golden colour. Do not overcook. Unlike the softer Greek cheeses halloumi becomes tough and overly chewy when cooked too long.

Cut into strips and serve immediately on warm plates, sprinkled with the vinaigrette.

Grilled stuffed mushrooms

Bruschetta

Makes 24

2 tablespoons lemon juice
1 tablespoon lime juice or dry white wine
24 large mushrooms
100ml (3^1/$_2$fl oz) extra virgin olive oil
6 shallots, finely chopped
1 medium red pepper, de-seeded and finely chopped
4 large garlic cloves, crushed
2 tablespoons finely chopped fresh flatleaf parsley
75g (2oz) fresh white breadcrumbs
50g (2oz) butter, melted
garlic salt and freshly ground black pepper

To make the marinade, whisk the lemon and lime juice or wine together in a shallow dish.

Remove the stalks from the mushrooms and finely chop. Place the caps in the marinade, cover the bowl, and leave in a cool place for 2–3 hours. Turn the mushrooms occasionally. Drain the mushrooms and reserve the remaining marinade.

Prepare the barbecue for grilling, following the instructions on **page 12**.

Heat the oil, either in a frying pan or on the barbecue's griddle plate, and sauté the shallots, red pepper, chopped mushroom stalks and garlic over medium heat for about 5 minutes or until the shallots have softened. Remove from the heat and transfer to a bowl. Mix in the parsley along with 4 tablespoons of the reserved marinade. Mix in the breadcrumbs and season to taste with the garlic salt and pepper.

Brush the tops of the mushroom caps with the melted butter and place upside down on the grill or griddle plate. Lightly fill the caps with the prepared stuffing and cook for about 10 minutes until well heated through.

Serve immediately.

The perfect appetiser for a gathering of garlic devotees.

Serves 4

1 French stick or day-old ciabatta loaf
4 large garlic cloves (use 1 clove for every 2–3 slices of bread)
extra virgin olive oil
salt and freshly ground black pepper

Prepare the barbecue for grilling, following the instructions on **page 12.**

Cut the bread into thick slices and toast over high heat. Rub one side of each toasted slice with garlic. Drizzle plenty of oil over the slices and season to taste with salt and pepper.

Crispy-griddled aubergine wedges

Makes 8–12

2 medium aubergines
75g (3oz) plain flour
25g (1oz) cornflour
1 tablespoon groundnut oil
25g (1oz) butter
salt

Peel the aubergines (I find a thin-bladed sharp, serrated knife is best for this task) and cut into quarters lengthways. If the aubergines are large, cut into 5 or 6 segments. Place the wedges, cut sides up, on a large plate and sprinkle with salt. Sit another large plate on the wedges and weigh down with something heavy. Set aside for 30–40 minutes before thoroughly rinsing the wedges under cold running water. Pat dry with kitchen paper.

Prepare the barbecue for grilling, following the instructions on **page 12**.

Blend the flours together in a bowl. Toss the wedges in the flour to coat them all over, shaking off any excess flour.

If the barbecue has a griddle plate, allow it to get hot before melting the oil and butter together. Otherwise use a heavy-based frying pan or skillet placed directly on the barbecue grill to heat the oil and butter. Cook the wedges for about 2 minutes on each side over medium heat until nicely browned and crisp all over. Serve immediately as they will tend to 'deflate' if left overlong.

 Serving Suggestion: If you like, you can serve the aubergines with a simple dip. Blend either 2 teaspoons of hot curry powder (or 1 tablespoon of curry paste) or 1 teaspoon of Dijon mustard, plus 1 tablespoon of tarragon or balsamic vinegar, into 150ml (1/4 pint) of mayonnaise (see page 133). Taste and adjust the seasoning as necessary.

Spicy cheesy potato slices

Olive bacon titbits

One of the tastiest, and undoubtedly one of the most economical appetisers around.

Makes about 40

4 large baking potatoes
75g (3oz) butter, softened
1 tablespoon barbecue seasoning
1/2 teaspoon garlic salt
25g (1oz) freshly grated Parmesan cheese

Prepare the barbecue for grilling, following the instructions on **page 12**.

Cut the potatoes lengthways into slices about 5mm (1/4 inch) thick, discarding the outer slices. Dry the slices with kitchen paper.

Mix together the butter, barbecue seasoning and garlic salt.

Brush the slices generously with half of the spicy butter and then cook, butter sides down, on the grill or griddle plate or grill over high heat for 4–5 minutes. Turn and baste the uncooked side with the remaining butter. Cook for a further 3–4 minutes or until the potato slices feel soft when pierced with a skewer. Sprinkle the Parmesan over the slices soon after turning.

 Serving Suggestion: To serve individual slices as an appetiser, pierce the edge of each slice with two wooden cocktail sticks, roughly 1cm (1/2 inch) apart. Bringing the ends of the sticks together will enable one to hold and eat the slice decorously.

Makes 24

12 rashers of streaky bacon
24 large green olives, stoned

Soak 24 bamboo skewers or wooden cocktail sticks in water. Prepare the barbecue for grilling following the instructions on **page 12**.

Cut the bacon rashers in half and grill until partially cooked but still flexible. Wrap each olive in a piece of bacon and thread it onto a skewer. Alternatively, secure each bacon-wrapped olive with a wooden cocktail stick.

Grill over medium to high heat for about 10 minutes or until the bacon is crisp and nicely browned. Turn the titbits occasionally during cooking.

Grilled prawns piquant

Serves 6–8

1kg (2 lb) raw Dublin Bay or Pacific prawns, shells snipped open along the back, de-veined and rinsed in cold running water

For the marinade:
3 tablespoons olive oil
3 tablespoons chopped fresh parsley
juice of 1 lemon
2 tablespoons hot pepper sauce (or to taste)
3 garlic cloves, very finely chopped
1 tablespoon tomato purée
2 teaspoons salt
1 teaspoon freshly ground black pepper
2 teaspoons dried oregano

To make the marinade, mix together the ingredients in a bowl. Put a little aside in a dish and place in the refrigerator. Place the remainder in a strong plastic bag together with the prepared prawns. Seal the bag and refrigerate for 2–3 hours.

Soak 10–12 bamboo skewers in water. Prepare the barbecue for grilling, following the instructions on **page 12**.

Drain the prawns, discarding the marinade, and thread 3 or 4 onto each skewer.

Place on the grill or griddle plate, and cook over medium heat for 4–5 minutes per side or until the prawns curl and begin to change to a light pink colour. Baste frequently with the reserved marinade. Do not overcook – unless you like your prawns chewy! Serve hot.

Prawns with a hint of mint & garlic

Served hot from the grill, these flavourful prawns make delicious appetisers.

Serves 6–8

1kg (2 lb) raw tiger prawns, peeled, de-veined and rinsed in cold running water

For the marinade:
1 large or 2 medium garlic cloves, crushed
1^1/$_2$ tablespoons chopped fresh mint
1 teaspoon salt
^{1}/$_4$ teaspoon freshly ground black pepper
1 teaspoon chilli powder
1 tablespoon red or white wine vinegar
1 tablespoon chopped fresh basil
150ml (^{1}/$_4$ pint) olive oil

To make the marinade, mix together the ingredients in a bowl. Add the prawns and turn until well coated with the marinade. Cover and refrigerate for 5–7 hours or overnight.

Soak 10–12 bamboo skewers in water. Prepare the barbecue for grilling, following the instructions on **page 12**.

Briefly drain the prawns and reserve the marinade. Thread the prawns onto the skewers and place on the grill or griddle plate. Cook over medium heat for 4–5 minutes, turning once and basting frequently with the marinade. Do not overcook. Serve hot.

Scallop & mushroom teriyaki

Makes 12

12 scallops out of their shells, washed and dried
4 tablespoons soy sauce
40g (1^1/$_2$oz) soft brown sugar
2 tablespoons groundnut or sunflower oil
1 tablespoon mirin or dry sherry
1 teaspoon freshly grated root ginger
1 garlic clove, crushed
12 closed-cap mushrooms, stalks removed

Soak 4 bamboo skewers in water. Prepare the barbecue for grilling, following the instructions on **page 12**.

Place the scallops in a bowl. Mix together the soy sauce, sugar, oil, mirin or sherry, ginger and garlic. Pour the mixture over the scallops, stir gently to coat and leave them to marinate for about 10 minutes. Remove the scallops, reserving the marinade.

Place a scallop in each mushroom cup and thread three onto each skewer, taking care that the scallops are held securely. Grill over medium to high heat for about 5 minutes or until the scallops are opaque and firm. Turn and baste frequently with the reserved marinade. Serve immediately.

Wing drumsticks teriyaki

Barbecued beef morsels

Makes 20

20 meaty chicken wings

For the teriyaki marinade:
1¹/₂ tablespoons clear honey
1¹/₂ tablespoons groundnut or sunflower oil
4 tablespoons soy sauce
1 tablespoon red wine or red wine vinegar
1 teaspoon freshly grated root ginger
1 large garlic clove, crushed

Mix together all the ingredients for the marinade.

Cut through the wing joints and either discard the pointed tips or freeze and use for for grilling as appetiser titbits, if liked.

Using a small sharp knife, carefully loosen the flesh around the lower joints of the remaining wing portions and push down so that they resemble mini-lollipops. Place these prepared wing drumsticks in a bowl and pour over the marinade. Cover with cling film and leave for 2–3 hours in a cool place, or overnight in the refrigerator, turning the wings occasionally.

Prepare the barbecue for 'Indirect heat' cooking, following the instructions on **page 14**.

Drain the wing drumsticks and reserve the marinade. Cook on the barbecue with medium to high heat, with the lid down, for 20–30 minutes, or until cooked and a dark golden/mahogany colour. (Basting frequently with the reserved marinade will result in the drumsticks taking on a dark mahogany hue.)

> **Note:** If you prefer to grill the wing drumsticks over direct heat, reduce the cooking time to about 15 minutes and baste the chicken occasionally with some of the reserved marinade.

Makes about 40

1kg (2 lb) sirloin of beef, cut into bite-size pieces

For the marinade:
5cm (2 inch) piece of fresh root ginger
2 small onions, chopped
¹/₂ teaspoon crushed garlic
125g (4oz) sugar
6 small dried chilli peppers or 1 teaspoon chilli powder
2 tablespoons red wine vinegar
4 teaspoons cornflour

To make the marinade, mix the ginger, onions, garlic, sugar, chilli and vinegar in a small pan and cook over a low heat for about 20 minutes or until slightly thickened. Blend the cornflour with 150ml (¹/₄ pint) cold water. Gradually add to the pan and keep stirring until the mixture is clear. Pass the marinade through a sieve into a bowl, pressing out all the juices. Discard the pulp and allow the marinade to cool.

Add the beef to the marinade, cover and allow to stand for 4–6 hours.

One hour before you intend to cook, soak 20 bamboo skewers in cold water. Prepare the barbecue for grilling, following the instructions on **page 12**.

Thread 2 to 3 pieces of meat onto each skewer and grill over medium to high heat, turning and basting frequently with the remaining marinade, for about 10 minutes or until the beef is cooked to your preference.

fish & shellfish

Grilled lobster; Stir-fried Szechuan prawns; Griddled coquille St Jacques with coriander & lime butter; Special baked scallops; Mushroom & scallop kebabs; Angels on horseback; Mussels with herb & garlic stuffing; Grilled oysters with garlic butter; Smoky grilled mussels; Sardines asadas with herb & garlic butter; Baked whole fish; Spicy lime sardines; Grilled red mullet with fennel; Grilled herrings with apple & cheese stuffing; Herrings grilled with fresh herbs; Swordfish steaks à la niçoise; Grilled halibut with a lemon-basil vinaigrette; Fish steaks with sweet & sour sauce; Grilled salmon steaks; Eric's griddled fish cakes; Grilled spicy trout with salsa; Tickled trout; Graham's smoky mountain trout; Jens-Jacob's hinged salmon fillets with piquant sauce; Parmesan mackerel; Tandoori fish.

Grilled lobster

Fresh lobster is available during the spring/summer months. Females not only make better eating but also provide the coral for making delicious coral butter. This recipe is in the 'unashamed luxury' class.

Serves 2

2 live female lobsters, each weighing about 500g (1 lb)
175g (6oz) butter
1 teaspoon paprika
salt and freshly ground black pepper
1 lemon, cut into wedges, to serve

Place the lobsters in the freezer for 2–3 hours to send them to sleep before you kill them. Kill the lobsters by laying them on their backs and inserting the tip of a sharp knife between the body shell and tail segment – thus severing the spinal cord. Otherwise, plunge each lobster head first into vigorously boiling water, using tongs to hold it under the surface for 2–3 minutes (the lobster will begin to turn red).

Prepare the barbecue for grilling, following the instructions on **page 12**.

Place the lobsters on a chopping board and split each one lengthways by drawing a sharp knife down the centre of the back. Discard the black intestine running down the middle of the tail and the white gills from the top of the head. Remove the bright red coral or roe and set aside.

Mix together 50g (2oz) of the butter, the paprika and a pinch each of salt and pepper. Spread over the lobster flesh.

Grill the lobster halves, cut sides down, over medium to medium-high heat, for 5–7 minutes. Turn the halves and cook for another 10 minutes or so. (By doing this the lobster's shell will retain most of the meat juices.) The lobster is ready to eat when the tail meat becomes opaque.

Blend the remaining butter with the reserved coral. Serve the lobsters with the coral butter and lemon wedges.

Stir-fried Szechuan prawns

Serves 2

500g (1 lb) raw tiger prawns
2 spring onions, roughly chopped
2 x 2.5cm (1 inch) pieces of fresh root ginger, peeled and crushed
50g (2oz) mangetout or French beans, cut into 5cm (2 inch) lengths
1/2 teaspoon sesame oil
3 tablespoons rice wine or dry sherry
1 teaspoon sugar
6 tablespoons soy sauce
1 dried red chilli, de-seeded and crushed
2 tablespoons groundnut oil

Pull the legs from the prawns. De-vein the prawns by carefully slitting the shell down the back (I find kitchen scissors are best for this task) and remove the black thread-like vein. Try not to dislodge the shell whilst doing this. Rinse the prawns quickly in cold water and pat dry.

Combine all the remaining ingredients, except the groundnut oil, in a dish. Add the prawns to the marinade, cover with cling film, and leave in the refrigerator for 2–3 hours, stirring occasionally.

Prepare the barbecue for wok-cooking, following the instructions on **page 19**. Remove the prawns from the marinade, drain and pat dry with kitchen paper. Reserve the marinade.

Heat the wok on the barbecue and add the groundnut oil. When the oil is hot, add the prawns and stir-fry over high heat for 3–4 minutes. The prawns are done when they turn a pink colour; take care not to overcook.

Add the reserved marinade to the prawns and bring rapidly to the boil. Serve immediately.

Griddled coquille St Jacques with coriander & lime butter

Griddled scallops will make a delicious, if extravagant, light main course for that special 'barbecue à deux'. Bon appetit.

Serves 2

2 tablespoons chopped fresh coriander leaves
50g (2oz) butter, at room temperature
juice of 1 lime
10 large scallops

Blend the coriander, butter and lime juice together.

Prepare the barbecue for grilling, following the instructions on **page 12**.

Melt the coriander and lime butter on the barbecue's griddle plate, or in a large heavy-based grill pan. Place the scallops about 5cm (2 inches) apart on the griddle plate or in the grill pan, and cook over a medium to high heat for 4–5 minutes until firm, occasionally spooning some of the melted herby butter over the scallops. Test regularly over the last 2–3 minutes of cooking as they can easily overcook.

 Serving suggestion: Serve with a tomato salad and some baby new potatoes.

Special baked scallops

Serves 4

25g (1oz) butter, melted
6 large scallops, removed from their shells, 4 of the shells washed and dried
juice of 1 lemon
5 tablespoons double cream
3 tablespoons fresh white breadcrumbs
salt and freshly ground black pepper

Prepare the barbecue for 'Indirect heat' cooking following the instructions on **page 14**.

Put 1 teaspoon of the melted butter in the bottom of each shell. Quarter the scallops and place 6 pieces in each shell. Season with salt and pepper and add a good squeeze of lemon juice. Spoon over the cream and sprinkle with the breadcrumbs. Dribble the rest of the melted butter over the breadcrumbs.

Bake over medium to medium-high heat for 8–10 minutes or until the tops are golden brown. Serve immediately.

Mushroom & scallop kebabs

This is really just a buttery version of the teriyaki kebabs I've given on page 30, for those who prefer more traditional flavours.

Serves 2

12 large scallops
12 closed-cap or large button mushrooms, stalks removed
6 tablespoons melted butter
juice of 1 lemon
salt and freshly ground black pepper

Soak 4 bamboo skewers in water. Prepare the barbecue for grilling, following the instructions on **page 12**.

Place a scallop in each mushroom and push a soaked skewer through the centre. Assemble 3 scallops and mushrooms on each skewer, leaving a gap of 2.5cm (1 inch) or so between them. Combine the melted butter and the lemon juice and brush this mixture generously over the kebabs. Lightly season with salt and pepper.

Grill over medium heat for about 8 minutes, or until the scallops have just turned opaque and are slightly firm to the touch. Do not overcook. Turn and baste the kebabs frequently with melted butter during cooking.

Pour any remaining butter into a small bowl and serve it with the kebabs.

Angels on horseback

Serves 4

8 canned or shelled raw oysters
1 tablespoon lemon juice
8 thin rashers of bacon
melted butter, for brushing
salt and freshly ground black pepper
4 slices of hot, buttered toast, to serve

Soak 8 wooden cocktail sticks in water. Prepare the barbecue for grilling, following the instructions on **page 12**.

Sprinkle the oysters with the lemon juice, salt and pepper. Wrap each oyster in a bacon rasher and fasten with a cocktail stick.

Brush the skewered oysters with the melted butter and grill over medium to medium-high heat for about 3–4 minutes, turning several times. Do not overcook.

Serve immediately, with the prepared toast.

Mussels with herb & garlic stuffing

A golden opportunity to ask the cook to 'show us your mussels'.

Serves 4

40–60 mussels
125g (4oz) butter, at room temperature
1 heaped tablespoon chopped fresh parsley
2 garlic cloves, crushed
1 tablespoon lemon juice
2 tablespoons dry white wine (optional)
salt and freshly ground black pepper

Place the mussels under cold running water for at least 30 minutes. Scrape away any weed and then clean by scrubbing with a small stiff brush.

Prepare the barbecue for grilling, following the instructions on **page 12**.

Put the prepared mussels into a large, heavy-bottomed pan. Cover the pan with its lid, place the pan on the grill and cook over medium heat until the mussels are fully open (you don't need to add liquid at this stage). Remove and discard the empty half shells and any mussels that have failed to open.

Whilst the mussels are cooking, combine the butter, parsley, garlic, lemon juice, wine (if using) and salt and pepper in a basin and mix well.

Prepare the barbecue for 'Indirect heat' cooking, following the instructions on **page 14**.

Arrange the mussels, in their half shells, on a baking tray. Spoon a small amount of the butter mixture onto each mussel and cook over medium to medium/high heat for about 5 minutes.

Serve immediately with chunks of fresh bread to mop up the juices.

Smoky grilled mussels

Mussels are a very great favourite of mine, to such an extent that for me the words 'moule' and 'drool' are synonymous! Do try out this simple, inexpensive and delicious recipe before standing down your barbecue at summer's end as it might encourage you to repeat the exercise throughout the winter. Mussels are best eaten on the day of purchase, but if you have to keep them overnight, do so (having washed and scrubbed them) in a bucket full of salted water. Sprinkle some fine oatmeal over the water and leave the bucket in a cool place covered with a damp tea towel.

Serves 4

40–60 mussels
large bunch of dried herbs, e.g. rosemary and thyme
1 quantity of Herb and garlic butter (page 164) or
Garlic butter (page 163), melted

Place the mussels under cold running water for at least 30 minutes. Scrape away any weed and clean the mussels by scrubbing with a small stiff brush.

Prepare the barbecue for grilling, following the instructions on **page 12**.

Place the mussels in a single layer on the grill and cook over medium to medium/high heat. Scatter the dried herbs onto the hot rocks throughout the short cooking period (keeping the lid closed will enhance the effect of the scented smoke on the aromatic flavour of the mussels). When the mussels have opened fully, leave them on the grill for another minute. Discard any mussels whose shells have failed to open.

Serve immediately, with your choice of melted Herb and garlic butter or Garlic butter.

Grilled oysters with garlic butter

Before buying your oysters, I strongly recommend that you are in possession of, or can borrow, an oyster-shucking knife.

Serves 4

24 oysters in their shells
250g (8oz) butter
2 teaspoons very finely chopped garlic
3 tablespoons very finely chopped fresh parsley
juice of 1 lemon

Scrub the oysters well and keep them, flat shell uppermost, covered with a damp cloth in a bucket until ready to cook. Do not store in water.

Prepare the barbecue for grilling, following the instructions on **page 12**.

Mix together the butter, garlic, parsley and lemon juice in a saucepan and place so the mixture simmers gently on the grill just before cooking the oysters.

Open the oysters and sever the meat from their shells. Add a teaspoonful or so of the garlic butter to each oyster.

Place the shells in a single layer on the grill and cook over high heat until the juices in the shells are bubbling and the oysters beginning to shrink. (The exact cooking time will depend on personal preference, but overcooking will result in the oysters becoming chewy.)

Serve immediately.

Sardines asadas with herb & garlic butter

To impart that little bit of extra oceanic flavour to the cleaned sardines, bury them in coarse salt and leave to cure for 2–3 hours. Brush off most of the salt before you oil, season and grill the fish. Frozen sardines may be used, but thaw them thoroughly beforehand.

Serves 4

20 small fresh sardines, cleaned
4 tablespoons olive oil
salt and freshly ground black pepper
1 quantity of Herb and garlic butter (page 164), to serve

Prepare the barbecue for grilling, following the instructions on **page 12**.

Pat the sardines dry. Brush lightly with the oil and season to taste with salt and pepper. Place the sardines on the grill and cook over high heat for about 3–4 minutes on each side.

Serve the sardines with the Herb and garlic butter.

Baked whole fish

This recipe is particularly suitable for sea bass, salmon or red mullet.

Serves 6–12

1 whole fish, weighing 1.75–3kg (4–7 lb), cleaned and scaled
4 spring onions, very finely chopped
1 teaspoon salt
1 teaspoon sugar
1 teaspoon freshly grated root ginger
1 tablespoon soy sauce
1 tablespoon sake, dry sherry or dry wine
1 tablespoon groundnut or 2 teaspoons sesame oil, plus extra for brushing

Wipe the fish inside and out with a damp cloth and pat dry with kitchen paper. Remove the fins but leave the head and tail intact. Score the fish, almost to the bone, with 3 parallel diagonal slashes on each side.

Combine the spring onions, salt, sugar, ginger, soy sauce, sake, sherry or wine and chosen oil. Rub the fish inside and out with this mixture. Allow the fish to stand in a cool place for 30 minutes.

Prepare the barbecue for 'Indirect heat' cooking, following the instructions on **page 14**.

If you have a wire fish holder (see page 171) large enough to accommodate the fish, brush the inside with oil before enclosing the fish. Alternatively, make a foil pan (see page 170) large enough to take the fish. Brush the inside surface of the pan with oil before adding the fish.

Cook the fish over medium to high heat. If using a fish holder, allow 10 minutes' total cooking time for every 2.5cm (1 inch) of the fish's thickness (at its thickest point). Allow 2–3 extra minutes per 2.5cm (1 inch) if cooking the fish in a foil pan. Brush frequently with oil during cooking and carefully turn the fish halfway through. When the fish is done, the skin will be nicely browned and the flesh easily flaked with a fork. Do not overcook.

Spicy lime sardines

Try serving these delicious small fish on fresh crusty bread, allowing the juices from the sardines to soak in for a minute or so before eating

Serves 4

8–12 fresh sardines
1 tablespoon salt
4 limes
1 green chilli, de-seeded and finely sliced
100g (3½oz) fresh coriander leaves, roughly chopped
4 tablespoons olive oil

Prepare the barbecue for grilling, following the instructions on **page 12**.

Clean the sardines by cutting them open along the belly from just below the head to the tail. Scrape out the insides with a knife.

Rinse the sardines well under cold running water. Pat dry with kitchen paper. Sprinkle the insides with the salt.

Grate the zest from 1 lime and squeeze its juice into a small bowl. Cut a second lime into thin slices and set aside. Combine the lime juice, lime zest and chilli in a bowl.

Lightly slash both sides of each sardine in 3 or 4 places. Rub the lime and chilli mixture inside and over each fish.

Place the sardines in a shallow dish. Scatter the coriander over them. Place the reserved lime slices over the coriander and refrigerate for 1 hour.

Brush some of the oil over the inside of a wire fish holder (see page 171), if using, and on both sides of the sardines. Discard the lime slices and place the fish in the holder or on the grill.

If no holder is available, for ease of handling I suggest you use a pair (2 pairs if serving more than 8 sardines) of long flat-bladed skewers to impale several fish in one go. Impale the first skewer just below the head and the second skewer just above the tail. Alternate the sardines head to tail on the parallel blades.

Cook the sardines for 3–4 minutes on each side. Baste with the remaining oil frequently during cooking.

Serve with wedges cut from the two remaining limes.

Grilled red mullet with fennel

The marvellous flavour of the red mullet will be enhanced if you leave the livers inside them during cooking. Once the fish are cooked the liver can be extracted carefully and then pounded with a tablespoon of chopped capers, a tablespoon of chopped oregano and 3–4 tablespoons of olive oil. This mixture makes a very tasty salad dressing. To further increase the aromatic flavour of the fish, try placing a handful of dried fennel stalks on the hot rocks just before you commence cooking. The scented smoke from the fennel stalks will help to stimulate the appetites of neighbours down-wind, and of course your guests!

Serves 4

4 large or 8 small red mullet

For the marinade:
1 tablespoon melted butter
2 tablespoons olive oil
1/2 teaspoon black peppercorns, cracked
2 tablespoons dry white or red wine
2 garlic cloves, chopped finely
3 large bay leaves, each broken into 4 pieces
1 tablespoon chopped fresh fennel leaves

Clean the mullet, but leave the livers intact. Make 2 deep slashes on each side of each fish. Mix together the marinade ingredients and pour over the fish. Marinate for about 1 hour.

Prepare the barbecue for grilling, following the instructions on **page 12**.

Drain the mullet, reserving the marinade, and grill over medium to high heat for 5–8 minutes on each side, depending on the size and thickness of the fish. Baste each side twice during cooking, with the reserved marinade.

Grilled herrings with apple & cheese stuffing

Serves 4

Happily herrings are in shimmering peak condition when the time comes for summer cookouts. They take well to grilling, especially since they are best when thoroughly cooked.

4 fresh herrings, cleaned
50g (2oz) butter or margarine
1 small onion, finely chopped
1 dessert apple, coarsely grated
50g (2oz) Cheddar cheese, grated
25g (1oz) fresh white breadcrumbs
grated zest of 1/2 orange
4 tablespoons orange juice
oil for brushing
salt and freshly ground black pepper
orange wedges and parsley, to garnish

Soak 8 wooden cocktail sticks in water. Prepare the barbecue for grilling, following the instructions on **page 12**.

Scrape the herrings to remove all the scales. Discard the heads and trim the tails. Make 3 diagonal slashes across each side of each fish.

Melt 25g (1oz) of the butter in a small saucepan. Add the onion and cook until it softens and becomes translucent. Stir the apple, cheese, breadcrumbs and orange zest into the onion and season well with salt and pepper. Allow to cool slightly.

Stuff each herring with the apple and cheese mixture and secure each slit with 1 or 2 cocktail sticks.

Melt the remaining butter in a small saucepan and stir in the orange juice.

Place the herrings directly on the grill or in a wire fish holder (see page 171) that has been brushed with oil. Cook over medium-high heat for 5–8 minutes on each side until the skin is crisp and the flesh flakes easily. Baste frequently with the orange butter during grilling.

Remove the cocktail sticks and serve the herrings with a garnish of orange wedges and parsley.

Herrings grilled with fresh herbs

This dish is delicately flavoured, but beware of the bones. So do keep in mind that profound old Spanish saying, 'Telling lies and eating fish requires great care!'

Serves 4

4 medium-size fresh herrings, cleaned
125g (4oz) butter
1/4 teaspoon ground cardamom
1/2 teaspoon ground coriander
1/2 teaspoon salt
a good pinch of freshly ground black pepper
300ml (1/2 pint) natural yoghurt
oil for brushing
sprigs of fresh fennel, dill or thyme

Scrape the herrings to remove all the scales. Discard the heads and trim the tails. Make 3 diagonal slashes across each side of each fish. Pat the fish dry with kitchen paper.

Prepare the barbecue for grilling, following the instructions on **page 12**.

Melt the butter in a small saucepan and stir in the cardamom, coriander, salt, pepper and yoghurt. Brush the fish generously, inside and out, with the seasoned butter.

Place the herrings in a wire fish holder (see page 171) that has been brushed with oil. (An oiled rectangular steak or hamburger grill will suffice, providing it is large enough to accommodate the fish.) Otherwise, place the fish directly on the grill or griddle plate.

Cook the fish over high heat for 5–8 minutes on each side until the skin is crisp and the flesh flakes easily with a fork. Baste frequently with the seasoned butter and occasionally place sprigs of your chosen herb on the fire-bed to enhance the aromatic flavour of the fish.

Heat any remaining seasoned butter and serve with the herrings.

Swordfish steaks à la niçoise

If swordfish is not available, substitute another firm-fleshed fish such as shark, halibut, turbot or cod.

Serves 4

4 x 250g (8oz) swordfish steaks
oil for brushing
lemon wedges, to serve
coarsely chopped fresh parsley, to serve

For the sauce:
4 tablespoons softened butter
2 tablespoons olive oil
2 garlic cloves, very finely chopped
2 anchovy fillets, soaked, drained and mashed
1 tablespoon finely chopped fresh parsley
3 black olives, stoned and finely chopped (optional)
juice of 1 lemon
freshly ground black pepper

Prepare the barbecue for grilling, following the instructions on **page 12**.

To make the sauce, melt the butter in a small saucepan. Add the oil, garlic, anchovy fillets, parsley, olives (if using) and lemon juice. Add pepper to taste. Cook over low to medium heat for 10 minutes, stirring occasionally. Keep the pan over very low heat until ready to use.

Brush the swordfish steaks with oil and grill over high heat for 5–10 minutes per side, depending on the thickness of the steaks. Take care not to overcook.

Pour the sauce evenly over the steaks and garnish with the lemon wedges and chopped parsley.

Grilled halibut with a lemon-basil vinaigrette

Serves 4

4 x 250g (8oz) halibut steaks
oil for brushing
salt and freshly ground black pepper

For the vinaigrette:
2 tablespoons lemon juice
2 tablespoons olive oil
2 garlic cloves, very finely chopped
2 tablespoons fresh basil, torn into small pieces
2 teaspoons capers
1 teaspoon lemon zest

Combine all the ingredients for the vinaigrette. Allow to stand for an hour or so before commencing to cook.

Prepare the barbecue for grilling, following the instructions on **page 12**.

Brush the halibut steaks with oil and season with salt and pepper.

Cook the steaks over low to medium heat for 5–8 minutes on each side (taking care not to overcook). When cooked, drizzle the vinaigrette over and serve immediately. **Tomatoes provençale** (page 124) make a good accompaniment to the halibut.

Fish steaks with sweet & sour sauce

Serves 6

6 fresh or frozen halibut, haddock, cod or
swordfish steaks, 2.5cm (1 inch) thick
oil for greasing

For the sweet and sour sauce:
150ml ($1/4$ pint) dry white wine
2 tablespoons white wine vinegar
2 tablespoons olive oil
300ml ($1/2$ pint) crushed pineapple with juice
1 tablespoon soy sauce
2 teaspoons lemon juice
$1/2$ teaspoon mustard powder
$1/2$ teaspoon garlic salt
$1 1/2$ tablespoons brown sugar
1 tablespoon chopped onion (optional)
oil for brushing

Thaw the steaks, if frozen. Arrange the fish steaks in a shallow dish.

Mix together the ingredients for the sauce. Pour the sauce over the steaks, cover and leave in the refrigerator for 30 minutes, turning once.

Prepare the barbecue for grilling, following the instructions on **page 12**, or 'Indirect heat' cooking, following the instructions on **page 14**.

Briefly drain the fish and reserve the sauce. Place the fish steaks in a wire fish holder (see page 171) that has been brushed with oil (prior to placing on the grill), or on the griddle plate, and cook over medium heat for 5 minutes on each side or until the fish flakes easily with a fork, basting with the sauce several times during cooking.

Alternatively, arrange the steaks in a shallow baking tin, baste with the sauce and cook by the 'Indirect heat' method, allowing an extra 8–10 minutes total cooking time. Turn the steaks carefully about halfway through cooking and baste with the sauce.

Grilled salmon steaks

Serves 4

4 salmon steaks about 2.5cm (1 inch) thick
1 teaspoon very finely chopped onion
$1/2$ teaspoon paprika
a generous pinch of garlic salt
2 teaspoons lemon juice
oil or melted butter for brushing
salt and freshly ground white pepper

Wipe the fish with a damp cloth. Season both sides of the salmon steaks with salt and pepper.

Stir the onion, paprika, garlic salt and a little more pepper to taste, into the lemon juice. Brush both sides of the salmon steaks with the marinade and leave in a cool place for about 30 minutes. Drain briefly, reserving any liquid.

Prepare the barbecue for grilling, following the instructions on **page 12**.

If using a wire fish holder (see page 171), brush oil over the inside. Place the steaks in the holder and cook over medium to high heat for 5–6 minutes on each side, basting frequently with any leftover marinade. Otherwise, place the steaks directly on the grill or griddle plate.

Alternatively, tear off 4 pieces of 46cm (18inch) heavy-duty foil large enough to 'wrap' each steak. Brush melted butter all over the shiny side of each piece of foil. Place a marinated salmon steak in the centre of the buttered surface. Having spooned a little of the marinade over the fish, bring the 2 long sides of the foil together above the steak. Fold over twice (leaving some space above the steak to allow for heat circulation and expansion); then fold the short ends in the same way to make a fairly leakproof package. Place the foil packages on the grill or griddle plate and cook over medium to high heat for about 10 minutes on each side or until the fish flakes easily with a fork.

Eric's griddled fish cakes

This recipe should appeal to those readers who, like me, have fond memories of school-canteen fish cakes. Despite their 'armour-plated' exteriors (possibly due to the previous day's batch being refried?) they were always very tasty. For this recipe you can use any fish you like, such as haddock, cod, sea bass, red mullet, etc., but salmon does give the cakes that little extra richness and elan.

Serves 6 as a main course, 10 as a starter and approximately 24 as an appetiser

300g (10oz) potatoes
425g (14oz) fish, filleted, boned and skinned
3 tablespoons lime juice
2 tablespoons chopped fresh coriander leaves
1 tablespoon chopped fresh basil (optional)
1 tablespoon capers, roughly chopped
$1/4$ teaspoon cayenne pepper
garlic salt, to taste
3 tablespoons groundnut oil
40g (1$1/2$oz) butter

Wash the potatoes, leaving the skins intact. Boil in lightly salted water for 10–12 minutes for medium-size potatoes, if using small, new potatoes allow 8–10 minutes. Do not overcook. Drain the potatoes and, when cool enough to handle, peel off the skins. Grate the potatoes, using the large holes of the grater, into a large bowl.

Chop the fish into very small chunks and add to the grated potato along with the lime juice, coriander, basil (if using) and capers. Mix well, but gently (trying not to break up the fish chunks too much), and season with the cayenne pepper and garlic salt.

Take spoonfuls of the mixture and firmly press into the desired cake size.

Prepare the barbecue for grilling, following the instructions on **page 12**.

If your barbecue incorporates a griddle plate, allow it to get hot before applying the oil and butter. Otherwise use a heavy-based frying pan placed directly on the grill. Fry the fish cakes over medium heat for 3–4 minutes on each side depending upon their size and thickness. You should end up with crusty, golden fish cakes. Drain on kitchen paper and serve immediately.

Grilled spicy trout with salsa

Tickled trout

Serves 4

4 x 250g (8oz) trout, cleaned
2 tablespoons ground cumin
1 tablespoon ground coriander
juice of 1/2 lemon
1 tablespoon olive oil
salt and freshly ground black pepper

For the salsa:
2 tablespoons fresh coriander leaves, chopped
250g (8oz) ripe tomatoes, de-seeded and diced
1 small red onion, very finely chopped
juice of 1/2 lemon
salt and freshly ground black pepper

Mix the salsa ingredients together and adjust the seasoning to taste. Set aside for the flavours to blend.

Cut 5 diagonal slashes in each side of each trout. Mix the ground cumin, ground coriander and some salt together and rub the mixture all over the trout, making sure it goes into the slashes. Leave in a cool place for about 20 minutes.

In the meantime prepare the barbecue for grilling, following the instructions on **page 12**.

Season the trout with salt, drizzle with the lemon juice and oil and place on the grill or griddle plate. Cook over medium heat for about 5 minutes on each side (follow the principle of allowing 10 minutes total cooking time per 2.5cm/1 inch of the fish's thickness). Serve with the salsa.

Tickling trout is no laughing matter for either the fish or the fisherman. The trout I tickled and caught as a very young boy, was all of 10cm (4 inches) long (and that is probably stretching things a little!).

Serves 4

4 x 375g (12oz) trout, cleaned and boned
oil for brushing
2 tablespoons melted butter
1 quantity of Maitre d'hotel butter (page 164), softened

For the marinade:
3 tablespoons olive oil
1 medium-sized onion, finely chopped
1 teaspoon Dijon mustard
1 tablespoon very finely chopped chives
2 tablespoons very finely chopped dill
1 teaspoon salt
1 teaspoon lemon juice
1/2 teaspoon freshly ground black pepper

Remove the heads from the trout. Cut down the back of each one and flatten out the fish. Place the trout flesh-side down in a shallow dish.

Thoroughly mix all the ingredients for the marinade in a small bowl. Pour this marinade over the fish, cover and refrigerate for about an hour, turning the fish once.

Prepare the barbecue for grilling, following the instructions on **page 12**.

Brush oil over the inner surfaces of a wire fish holder (see page 171) and place the trout, flesh sides down, in the holder or straight on the grill or griddle plate. Cook over medium heat for about 2 minutes. Turn the fish over and brush the melted butter over the cooked side. Continue grilling for a further 3–4 minutes, or until the skin is crisp and the flesh white and easily flaked with a fork. Do not overcook.

Spread the Maitre d'hotel butter over the trout just before serving.

Graham's smoky mountain trout

My old pal Graham Ducker, a very experienced barbecue cook, has long been a keen devotee of the 'pit barbecue' (with its smokestack, rather reminiscent of a steam engine) and the cigar-shaped 'smokers' (both units are reviewed on page 167). He reckons that trout, a prime freshwater fish for barbecuing, is even more delectable after taking a swim in a barbecue smoker. In Graham's recipe the bacon does the work of a fat-baster.

Serves 4

For the paste:
4 garlic cloves
juice of 1/2 lemon
1 teaspoon Worcestershire sauce
1 teaspoon freshly ground black pepper
1/2 teaspoon salt
1 teaspoon vegetable oil

4 x 250g (8oz) trout, cleaned and boned
8 rashers of bacon
6 tablespoons chopped onion
6 tablespoons chopped green pepper
6 tablespoons finely chopped celery
50g (2oz) dry white breadcrumbs
6 tablespoons chopped pecans

About 1 1/2 hours before you plan to barbecue, prepare the paste by mashing or chopping the garlic in a pestle and mortar or mini food processor. Mix in the lemon juice, Worcestershire sauce, pepper and salt. Then blend in the oil to make a paste. Rub each trout inside and out with the paste. Wrap the trout in cling film and refrigerate for about an hour.

Prepare the 'pit barbecue' (smoker) for barbecuing, or alternatively prepare a lidded charcoal or gas barbecue for 'smoke-cooking' (following the 'Indirect heat' cooking method on **page 14**). In the former case use well-seasoned logs of wood, such as beech, ash, sycamore or fruitwood. In the latter case use chips, or small chunks, of the above hardwoods, or oak, which will be more readily available at your local barbecue emporium. (See page 16 for further advice on smoke-cooking.) Whatever the type of barbecue you are using, bring the unit's cooking temperature to a low 60–70°C (140–160°F) on the heat indicator.

Remove the trout from the refrigerator and let them sit at room temperature for approximately 20 minutes. Soak 12–14 wooden cocktail sticks in water.

On the barbecue's griddle plate, or in a heavy skillet, fry the bacon over medium heat, removing it whilst it is still limp. Set the bacon aside. Add the onion, pepper and celery to the bacon drippings and sauté briefly until softened. Remove the mixture from the heat and stir in the breadcrumbs and pecans. Stuff each trout with a portion of this filling. Wrap 2 rashers of the partially cooked bacon around each fish, securing with cocktail sticks as needed.

Transfer the trout to the smoker, or lidded charcoal or gas barbecue, and cook until the bacon is browned and crisp and the fish opaque and easily flaked with a fork. This should take 40–50 minutes. Serve immediately.

 Graham's tip: Trout can take a heavier level of smoke-induced flavour than most fish, making them particularly suitable for the log-burning pit barbecues.

Jens-Jacob's hinged salmon fillets with piquant sauce

This recipe has been adapted from one kindly provided by an old friend, Jens-Jacob Andersen, a chef/restaurateur in Denmark. J-J informs me that the sauce is known in Denmark as 'Fox sauce'.

Serves 4

1 piece of salmon fillet (with the skin on but the bones removed), 20–30cm (8–12 inches) long, cut from the thick head to middle section of the fish
oil for brushing
salt and freshly ground black pepper

For the piquant dill sauce (Fox sauce):
2 tablespoons light brown sugar
2 tablespoons Dijon mustard
1 tablespoon oil
2 tablespoons fresh dill or 2 teaspoons dill weed
1/2 teaspoon salt
1/4 teaspoon freshly ground white pepper

Wipe the salmon fillet with a damp cloth. Season with salt and pepper. Cut the fillet crossways, into 4 equal pieces. Cut each piece across the centre of its width, down to the skin – taking care not to slice through the skin. Fold the sliced fillet pieces back on themselves, with the skin acting as a hinge.

Prepare the barbecue for grilling, following the instructions on **page 12**.

To make the sauce, first melt the sugar in about 2 tablespoons of boiling water. Combine the resulting syrup in a small bowl with the rest of the ingredients.

If using a hinged steak/burger holder (very useful for this recipe; see page 171), brush the inside well with oil before placing the hinged fillets inside. Otherwise place the fish directly on the grill or griddle plate. Brush the fillets with oil and cook over medium to high heat for 5–7 minutes per side depending upon the thickness of the 'salmon sandwich'. If the hinged fillets prove difficult to cook in an upright position simply cook them on their sides. Take care not to overcook. Serve immediately with a little of the sauce poured over the fish, and the remainder in a separate bowl.

Parmesan mackerel

Serves 4

4 x 300g (10oz) fresh mackerel
oil for greasing

For the marinade:
125ml (4fl oz) oil
4 tablespoons lemon juice
2 tablespoons chopped fresh parsley
1 teaspoon chopped fresh basil
1/2 teaspoon salt
1/4 teaspoon freshly ground white pepper
(if unavailable, black peppercorns will do)

For the coating:
75g (3oz) Parmesan cheese, grated
25g (1oz) dry white breadcrumbs
1/2 teaspoon garlic salt

Clean the mackerel and rinse thoroughly inside and out under cold running water. Wipe dry with kitchen paper. Place the fish side by side in a shallow dish.

Mix together the marinade ingredients. Pour the marinade over the mackerel, cover and keep in the refrigerator for 1 hour, turning the fish once or twice.

Prepare the barbecue for grilling, following the instructions on **page 12**.

Lift the mackerel from the marinade, drain briefly and reserve the marinade.

In a shallow dish combine the Parmesan, breadcrumbs and garlic salt. Thickly cover the mackerel with the cheese mixture, which should be pressed firmly onto the skin. Drizzle over some of the reserved marinade. Placing the mackerel in a wire fish holder (see page 171) that has been brushed with oil will help considerably with their handling. Regardless of whether or not you are utilising a fish holder, the fish should be placed directly on the grill or griddle plate and cooked over medium heat for about 5 minutes. Turn the fish and cook for a further 5–6 minutes or until the flesh flakes easily when prodded with a fork in the thickest part. Baste frequently with the reserved marinade during cooking.

Tandoori fish

Serves 2–3

75g (3oz) butter, melted
$^1/_2$ teaspoon ground nutmeg
$1^1/_2$ teaspoons ground cinnamon
$1^1/_2$ teaspoons ground coriander
juice of $1^1/_2$ lemons
1 whole white fish, around 1kg (2 lb),
e.g. haddock, cod or any other white,
firm-fleshed fish
1 medium onion, finely chopped
4 garlic cloves, very finely chopped
2.5cm (1 inch) piece of fresh root ginger, peeled
and finely chopped
1 teaspoon ground cumin
$^1/_4$ teaspoon chilli powder
1 teaspoon ground fennel
$^1/_2$ teaspoon paprika
1 teaspoon salt
$^1/_4$ teaspoon freshly ground black pepper
150ml ($^1/_4$ pint) natural yoghurt

First make the basting sauce. Combine the melted butter, nutmeg, $^1/_2$ teaspoon of the cinnamon, $^1/_2$ teaspoon of the coriander and the juice of half a lemon. Blend well and set aside.

Clean the fish; then make 3 diagonal slashes on each side.

Put the onion, garlic, ginger, cumin, remaining cinnamon and coriander, the chilli, fennel, paprika, salt, pepper and the remaining lemon juice in a food processor (or, preferably, use a pestle and mortar) and blend to make a paste. Stir in the yoghurt. Rub the mixture on the inside and outside of the fish and leave in a cool place for 3–4 hours.

Prepare the barbecue for spit-roasting, following the instructions on **page 17**, or grilling, following the instructions on **page 12**.

If you prefer to spit-roast the fish, it will be far easier to do so if you are in possession of a spit-mounted fish grill. If you prefer to grill the fish it will be a far easier task if you use a large, hinged wire fish holder (see page 171). Brush the inside of the holder with oil before enclosing the fish. If you do not possess a fish holder, place the fish directly on the grill or griddle plate.

Cook the fish over medium heat, basting frequently with the basting sauce, for 15 minutes if spit-roasting or 7–8 minutes per side if grilling. Bear in mind the fish grilling formula: allow a total cooking time of 10 minutes per 2.5cm (1 inch) thickness of fish e.g. if the fish is 5cm (2 inches) thick, cook each side for 10 minutes. Turning a large, partially cooked fish can be a somewhat delicate manoeuvre. I find that using 2 fish slices, each positioned a third of the way in from the tail or head, helps to keep the fish (and one's 'cool') intact.

poultry & game

Roast chicken with 'PUTS' (Pesto Under The Skin); Griddled chicken with crème fraîche & green peppercorns; Chicken with chilli glaze; Honsoywin chicken quarters; 'Quick-chick' tikka masala kebabs; Stir-fried five-spice chicken with lemon grass; Chicken satay with Indonesian sauce; Tandoori chicken; Stir-fried chicken with peppers in a sherry sauce; Sesame gingered chicken; Streaky drumsticks; Grilled poussins with mustard; Sweet & sour chicken; Grilled marinated quail; Orange burgundy duckling; Spit-roasted glazed duckling; Redskin wild duck; Christmas turkey; Teriyaki turkey drumsticks; Spit-roasted saddle or loin of venison; Venison steaks with cranberry & red wine sauce.

Roast chicken with 'PUTS' (Pesto Under The Skin)

In terms of vision and taste, this is a roast chicken with a difference. Inserting pesto under the skin is not difficult unless one's fingernails are excessively long and sharp. The skin of most chickens is remarkably supple and stretchy. Apart from the ridge of the breastbone (where you might have to gently use a short-bladed knife) and the knuckle ends of the drumsticks, the thin membrane that connects the skin to the flesh of the chicken is easily parted by gently working your fingers between them. Try to avoid breaking through the skin if you can, but the odd little tear is quite all right.

Serves 4–6

1.25–1.75kg (3–4 lb) chicken
(select one with its skin nicely intact)
groundnut oil for brushing
a handful of freshly grated Parmesan cheese

For the pesto:
3 tablespoons pine nuts or roasted hazelnuts
2 tablespoons freshly grated Parmesan cheese
2 garlic cloves, peeled
a handful of fresh basil leaves
2 tablespoons olive oil
1 egg yolk (optional)
50g (2oz) medium-fat soft cheese
salt and freshly ground black pepper

To make the pesto, place the pine nuts or roasted hazelnuts, Parmesan, garlic and basil in a food processor or blender. Process for about 20 seconds or so, then add the olive oil and egg yolk (if using). Continue processing until the mixture resembles a rough paste. Add the soft cheese and salt and pepper, then pulse (a few quick bursts of the processor) until the mixture blends together.

Using your hand, spread the pesto evenly under the skin of the chicken and over the meat. Brush the chicken with groundnut oil.

Prepare the barbecue for 'Indirect heat' cooking, following the instructions on **page 14**.

Roast the chicken with medium to high heat for about 1$\frac{1}{2}$ hours or until the juices run clear when a thigh is pierced with a skewer.

Scattering a little grated Parmesan over the oiled surface of the chicken after about an hour's cooking will produce an attractive light golden crust over the bird.

 Note: If in a hurry, purchase a jar of freshly prepared pesto from the deli counter of a supermarket – adding perhaps some extra ground pine nuts to give the pesto more body.

Griddled chicken with crème fraîche & green peppercorns

Serves 2

2 large chicken breasts, boned and skinned
200ml (7fl oz) crème fraîche
5 heaped teaspoons wholegrain mustard
2 heaped teaspoons bottled green peppercorns
1 heaped tablespoon chopped fresh parsley
groundnut oil for brushing
salt and freshly ground black pepper

Prepare the barbecue for grilling, following the instructions on **page 12**.

Pre-heat the grill, or allow the griddle plate to become very hot.

Brush the chicken breasts with a little oil and place on the grill or griddle plate. Cook on each side for 3–4 minutes or until the juices run clear.

Meanwhile tip the crème fraîche into a small saucepan and place over gentle heat on the edge of the barbecue grill or griddle plate. Stir in the mustard, peppercorns and parsley. Season to taste with salt and pepper.

Carry on bubbling down the sauce until it thickens slightly. This should take 3–4 minutes.

Serve the chicken breasts on warm plates, accompanied by the sauce. **Roasted potatoes with garlic, rosemary and thyme** (page 121) make an excellent vegetable accompaniment (see photograph, opposite).

Chicken with chilli glaze

As barbecue cooks our primary aim should be to produce food, be it a sausage or a steak, with the maximum possible appeal to all the senses, particularly sight and smell. Stimulating your guests' taste buds well before they get their teeth into the food will have a positive and beneficial effect on their appetites. This colourful, red-glazed chicken does just that and tastes good too!

Serves 4

4 tablespoons melted butter
1 teaspoon chilli powder
2 garlic cloves, very finely chopped
2 tablespoons lime juice
$1/4$ teaspoon grated lime zest
$1/4$ teaspoon ground cumin
1.25kg (3 lb) chicken, jointed

Prepare the barbecue for grilling, following the instructions on **page 12**.

Mix together the butter, chilli powder, garlic, lime juice and zest and cumin. Generously brush the chicken pieces with the mixture.

Place the chicken pieces, skin sides up, on the grill and grill over medium to high heat for about 40 minutes, turning the pieces and basting frequently, until the meat is cooked.

Honsoywin chicken quarters

A very tasty dish to set before your guests, but take care not to over-baste as this could make the skin overly dark and burnt. Aim for a deep-golden mahogany hue with a nicely lacquered finish.

Serves 4

4 chicken quarters

For the marinade:
4 tablespoons clear honey
4 tablespoons soy sauce
150ml (1/4 pint) white wine
150ml (1/4 pint) orange juice
1/4 teaspoon ground allspice
1 teaspoon paprika
1 garlic clove, crushed
2 tablespoons water

Place the chicken quarters in a dish.

To make the marinade, mix together all the ingredients. Pour the marinade over the chicken quarters, turning them to ensure an even coating. Cover the dish and leave in the refrigerator for a few hours or overnight; turn the pieces occasionally during this time.

Prepare the barbecue for grilling, following the instructions on **page 12**.

Drain the chicken pieces, reserving the marinade, and place on the grill. Cook over medium heat for 40–50 minutes or until fully cooked, basting with the marinade several times. To check that each quarter is cooked, pierce the thickest part with a skewer – the juices should run clear. If in any doubt, cut the meat to the bone in the thickest part, and check to see that the meat next to the bone is no longer pink.

'Quick-chick' tikka masala kebabs

A good-looking, delicious, 'fast-track' dish.

Serves 4

750g (1 1/2 lb) chicken breasts, boned and skinned
8 pitta breads, to serve
salt and freshly ground black pepper

For the marinade:
4 tablespoons tikka masala curry paste
150g (5oz) natural yoghurt

Cut each chicken breast into 5 or 6 pieces. Mix the curry paste with the yoghurt in a bowl and add the chicken pieces. Leave to marinate for about 30 minutes.

In the meantime, soak 4 bamboo skewers in water and prepare the barbecue for grilling, following the instructions on **page 12**.

Thread the chicken pieces onto the soaked bamboo skewers (you can use oiled metal ones if you wish) and season with salt and pepper. Place on the grill or griddle plate and cook over medium heat for 10–15 minutes or until the chicken is cooked through and beginning to char at the edges.

Serve with the pitta breads.

Stir-fried five-spice chicken with lemon grass

Serves 4–5

750g (1¹/₂ lb) chicken breasts, boned, skinned and thinly sliced
50g (2oz) finely chopped lemon grass
2 teaspoons grated fresh root ginger
2 garlic cloves, crushed
1¹/₂ tablespoons lime juice
1 teaspoon grated lime zest
1 teaspoon five-spice powder
60ml (2fl oz) soy sauce
2 tablespoons groundnut oil
250g (8oz) Chinese lettuce, shredded
8 spring onions, sliced
125g (4oz) bean sprouts
¹/₂ handful of fresh coriander leaves

Combine the chicken, lemon grass, ginger, garlic, lime juice and zest, five-spice powder and 1 tablespoon of the soy sauce in a large bowl. Cover the bowl and keep in a cool place for 3–4 hours or overnight in the refrigerator.

Prepare the barbecue for wok-cooking, following the instructions on **page 19**.

Place the wok on the barbecue and heat 1 tablespoon of the oil. Stir-fry the chicken mixture over high heat in small batches until all has been well browned and cooked through. Keep the cooked chicken in a dish adjacent to the barbecue to keep warm.

Heat the remaining oil and stir-fry the lettuce, onion and bean sprouts until the lettuce just begins to wilt.

Return the chicken mixture to the wok, along with the coriander and remainder of the soy sauce, and toss together to mix well.

Serving suggestion:
Serve on a bed of fine egg noodles.

Chicken satay with Indonesian sauce

Serves 4

1 quantity of Indonesian sauce (see page 162)
750g (1¹/₂ lb) chicken breasts, boned and skinned
groundnut oil for brushing
shredded lettuce, to serve

For the marinade:
1 garlic clove, crushed
2 tablespoons soy sauce
juice of 1 lemon

Prepare the Indonesian sauce 2 or 3 hours before cooking the chicken. Soak 8 bamboo skewers in water.

Cut the chicken into 2.5cm (1 inch) cubes. Mix together the marinade ingredients in a bowl and add the chicken cubes, turning to coat with the mixture. Cover the bowl and leave to marinate for about 30 minutes.

Prepare the barbecue for grilling, following the instructions on **page 12**.

Remove the chicken from the marinade and thread the cubes onto the soaked skewers. Re-heat the sauce gently, adding a little water if it is too thick. Brush the chicken with a little oil and grill, over medium heat, for about 6–8 minutes or until the chicken is cooked.

Serve the chicken on a dish lined with shredded lettuce and accompanied by the warm Indonesian sauce.

Tandoori chicken

In spite of the number of spices in this recipe, the end result is fairly mild. Excellent bottled tandoori paste is available in all supermarkets if you don't have the time or inclination to make your own.

Serves 6–8

3 x 1kg (2 lb) chickens
juice of 1^1/$_2$ lemons
melted ghee or groundnut oil for brushing
lemon wedges, to serve

For the tandoori marinade:
4 medium garlic cloves
1cm (^{1}/$_2$ inch) piece of fresh root ginger, peeled and chopped
1 teaspoon ground roasted cumin seeds
^{1}/$_2$ teaspoon ground cardamom
^{1}/$_2$ teaspoon ground cinnamon
^{1}/$_4$ teaspoon ground nutmeg
^{1}/$_2$ teaspoon chilli powder
^{1}/$_2$ teaspoon cayenne pepper
1 teaspoon salt
125ml (4fl oz) natural yoghurt

Cut the chickens into quarters and remove the wings from the breast pieces. Pull the skin from all the quarters (kitchen paper will help provide a better grip); then pierce the flesh all over with the point of a skewer or a sharp-pointed kitchen fork. Make deep diagonal slashes in the meat about 2.5cm (1 inch) apart.

Place the portions in a large bowl. Sprinkle over the lemon juice and rub in well for a minute or two. Cover the bowl and leave for 30 minutes.

For the tandoori marinade, put all the ingredients in a food processor or blender and blend until the mixture is smooth.

Pour the marinade over the chicken portions and mix thoroughly to coat well. Cover the bowl again and leave the chicken to marinate for at least 4 hours or overnight in the refrigerator. Remove the bowl from the refrigerator at least 1 hour before cooking to allow the chicken to come to room temperature.

Prepare the barbecue for grilling, following the instructions on **page 12**.

Place the chicken portions on the grill, bone sides down, and brush the slashed surface of the meat with melted ghee or oil. Cook over medium to high heat for about 10 minutes. Turn and baste the other sides and cook for a further 10 minutes. Continue to cook, turning and basting the chicken every 10 minutes until the meat is cooked – this will take 30–40 minutes.

Serve the chicken with the lemon wedges.

Stir-fried chicken with peppers in a sherry sauce

Serves 3–4

375g (12oz) chicken breasts, boned and skinned
1 teaspoon salt
2 teaspoons cornflour
3 tablespoons groundnut oil
1 medium green pepper, de-seeded
and cut into 2.5cm (1 inch) pieces
1 medium red pepper, de-seeded
and cut into 2.5cm (1 inch) pieces
2 dried red chilli peppers, de-seeded
and finely shredded

For the sherry sauce:
3 tablespoons chicken stock
2 tablespoons dry sherry
1 1/2 tablespoons red wine vinegar
or 1 tablespoon balsamic vinegar
1 tablespoon tomato purée
2 teaspoons cornflour

Slice the chicken breasts into small bite-size cubes. Sprinkle over the salt and cornflour and rub all together with 2 teaspoons of the oil. Combine the sauce ingredients in a bowl, mix well and set aside.

Prepare the barbecue for wok-cooking, following the instructions on **page 19**.

Heat the wok on the barbecue and add 1 tablespoon of the oil. When the oil is hot, add the chicken cubes and stir-fry over high heat for about 2 minutes or until the chicken has nicely browned. Remove the chicken to a bowl and keep warm adjacent to the barbecue. Add the remainder of the oil to the wok. When the oil is hot add the green and red peppers, chilli peppers and prepared sauce. Stir and cook until the sauce starts to boil before returning the chicken to the wok. Stir-fry for a further 2 minutes. Serve immediately.

Sesame gingered chicken

Serves 4

8 chicken thighs or drumsticks

For the marinade:
2.5cm (1 inch) piece of fresh root ginger,
peeled and grated
2 tablespoons sesame seeds
2 teaspoons sesame oil
1 tablespoon groundnut oil
1 garlic clove, very finely chopped
1/4 teaspoon cayenne pepper
25g (1oz) spring onion, finely chopped

Wash the chicken thighs or drumsticks, pat dry and pierce all over with the point of a skewer or sharp knife.

Combine the marinade ingredients and mix thoroughly. Brush the marinade all over the thighs or drumsticks and place in a dish. Cover the dish and leave in the refrigerator for a few hours or overnight.

Prepare the barbecue for grilling, following the instructions on **page 12**.

Lightly drain the thighs or drumsticks, reserving any marinade. Grill over medium to high heat for about 30 minutes or until nicely browned and cooked, turning and basting with the marinade a few times during cooking.

Streaky drumsticks

Serves 4

8 plump chicken drumsticks
75g (3oz) cream cheese
8 rashers of streaky bacon
groundnut or sunflower oil for basting
salt and freshly ground black pepper

Soak 8 wooden cocktail sticks in water. Prepare the barbecue for grilling, following the instructions on **page 12**.

Using a short, sharp knife, make a deep incision in the fattest part of each drumstick and fill the slit with cream cheese. Season with salt and pepper, then wrap a rasher of bacon around each drumstick and secure in place with a cocktail stick.

Grill over medium to high heat, basting frequently with oil, for about 12 minutes on each side or until cooked.

Grilled poussins with mustard

If you can't obtain poussins, very small chickens, about 375g (12oz) in weight, may be used instead. (Pictured opposite and on page 13.)

Serves 4

4 poussins
125ml (4fl oz) groundnut oil
1 tablespoon Dijon mustard
1 teaspoon dried rosemary
1 teaspoon dried thyme
2 bay leaves, crushed
dry white breadcrumbs for sprinkling
salt and freshly ground black pepper

Prepare the barbecue for grilling, following the instructions on **page 12**.

Split the poussins in half, from the back. Open them out and gently crush the bones by pressing down with the heel of your hand (or use a large heavy-bladed knife or cleaver) so that they lie flat while cooking. Season the poussins with salt and pepper.

Combine the oil, mustard, rosemary, thyme and bay leaves and mix well.

Brush some of the mixture over the poussins and grill them, bone sides down, over medium to high heat, for about 10 minutes. Turn and grill the other sides for 10–15 minutes or until cooked.

Brush the rest of the mustard mixture over the poussins and scatter with breadcrumbs. Return the poussins to the grill and cook for a further 2–3 minutes or until nicely browned.

Sweet & sour chicken

Serves 4

1.25–1.5kg (3–3¹/₂ lb) chicken
150ml (¹/₄ pint) soy sauce
200g (7oz) can of pineapple chunks
150ml (¹/₄ pint) chicken stock
2 garlic cloves, very finely chopped
1 tablespoon freshly grated root ginger
50g (2oz) brown sugar
3 tablespoons red or white wine vinegar
1 green pepper, de-seeded and cut
into 2.5cm (1 inch) squares
1 firm, ripe tomato, skinned,
de-seeded and chopped
4 spring onions, sliced diagonally
into 2.5cm (1 inch) pieces
2 tablespoons cornflour
3 tablespoons cold water

Using a heavy kitchen cleaver, joint and chop the chicken into 5cm (2 inch) pieces.

Combine the soy sauce, pineapple juice from the can, chicken stock, garlic, ginger, sugar and vinegar and mix well. Marinate the chicken pieces in the mixture in a cool place for 2–3 hours. Remove the chicken pieces from the marinade about 30 minutes before cooking. Reserve the marinade.

Prepare the barbecue for 'Indirect heat' cooking, following the instructions on **page 14**.

Brown the chicken pieces for about 15 minutes over the lit side of the barbecue. Transfer the part-cooked chicken to a deep-sided roasting tin. Arrange the pepper, tomato, pineapple chunks and spring onions around the chicken pieces and pour over the reserved marinade. Position the roasting tin over the unlit side of the barbecue and cook with low to medium heat for 30–40 minutes.

When the chicken pieces are cooked, remove them to a warm dish. Mix the cornflour with 3 tablespoons water to make a paste and stir this into the hot juices. Carefully move the roasting tin over to the lit side of the barbecue and simmer gently, stirring continuously, until the sauce has thickened.

Allow your guests to pour the hot sauce over the chicken. Serve with rice and a salad.

Grilled marinated quail

Unlike pheasant, quail should be eaten really fresh, preferably within 24 hours of being killed. This recipe calls for three quail per serving: two quail per head should still be adequate, but one quail per guest only stirs the appetite without satisfying it and brands the host as stingy.

Serves 4

12 quail, drawn and split lengthways
through the breastbone
125g (4oz) butter, melted

For the marinade:
600ml (1 pint) dry white wine
3 tablespoons lemon juice
1 1/2 tablespoons red or white wine vinegar
3 garlic cloves, crushed
1 teaspoon dried whole tarragon or rosemary leaves
1 teaspoon dried thyme
1 bay leaf
1 teaspoon salt
1/4 teaspoon freshly ground black pepper

To make the marinade, mix together the ingredients in a large saucepan and heat until simmering. Remove the pan from the heat, cover and allow to stand for 1–2 hours.

Pour the marinade into a dish and add the quail to the mixture, turning the birds a few times before covering the dish. Leave for 6–8 hours or overnight in the refrigerator.

Prepare the barbecue for grilling, following the instructions on **page 12**.

Remove the quail from the marinade, drain and then pat dry with kitchen paper. (Either discard the marinade or freeze it for future use.)

Grill the quail, cut sides down, over medium heat for about 15–20 minutes, turning them occasionally and basting when you do so with the melted butter. Serve immediately.

Orange burgundy duckling

Serves 4

1.75–2.25kg (4–5 lb) duckling
300ml (1/2 pint) red burgundy wine
1 teaspoon salt
1 teaspoon freshly ground black pepper
1/2 teaspoon dried thyme
1 orange, cut into quarters
2 slices of onion
leaves from 1 head of celery
150ml (1/4 pint) freshly squeezed orange juice

Prepare the barbecue for 'Indirect heat' cooking, following the instructions on **page 14**. (Use a drip pan.)

Remove any giblets from the duckling. Wash and pat dry, inside and out, with kitchen paper.

Brush the cavity of the duckling with a little of the wine and sprinkle with the salt, pepper and thyme. Place the orange, onion and celery leaves inside and close the cavity with fine skewers.

Mix together the remaining wine and the orange juice and use some to brush the outside of the duckling.

Roast the duckling with medium to high heat for about 2 hours or until tender, occasionally pricking the thighs and breast skin with a sharp skewer or small knife, and basting with the wine mixture after 30 minutes. Baste frequently during cooking.

Discard the flavourings in the cavity and cut the duckling into portions. Place the portions on a hot serving dish. If desired, skim the fat from the pan juices and pour the juices over the duckling before serving.

Spit-roasted glazed duckling

Serves 3–4

1.75–2.25kg (4–5 lb) plump young duckling
2 tablespoons clear honey

For the marinade:
4 tablespoons dry red wine
1 teaspoon soy sauce
2 tablespoons sugar
3 tablespoons groundnut oil
1 teaspoon paprika
1/2 teaspoon freshly grated root ginger
a pinch of ground cinnamon
a pinch of grated nutmeg
a pinch of freshly ground black pepper

Carefully wipe the duckling inside and out with a damp cloth and pat dry with kitchen paper.

Mix together the ingredients for the marinade. Spread the mixture over the inside and outside of the bird and wrap it completely in foil. Place the wrapped duckling in a refrigerator and leave for 24–36 hours. Remove it about 2 hours before cooking.

Prepare the barbecue for spit-roasting, following the instructions on **page 17**.

Remove the duckling from the foil, reserving the remaining marinade. Run a spit through the exact centre of the bird, firmly set the spit forks in the thighs and breast and test for balance (see page 18).

Position the spit on the barbecue and cook over medium heat if spit-roasting with the barbecue lid down, or over medium to high heat if open spit-roasting. Cook for about 1½ hours or until the thigh meat is soft when squeezed (protect your fingers with kitchen paper). Baste occasionally with the reserved marinade. Stir the honey into the marinade 15 minutes before the end of cooking and baste the duckling several times with the mixture so that the skin is richly glazed. Carve and serve immediately.

Redskin wild duck

Although game butchers will supply the ducks well hung and ready to cook, they still need to be carefully wiped, inside and out, with a slightly damp cloth just before cooking.

Serves 4–8

4 wild ducks, each 500g–1.1kg (1–2½ lb), well hung
125g (4oz) butter, softened
Worcestershire sauce, for coating
paprika, for sprinkling
1½ tablespoons cornflour
3 tablespoons port

Prepare the barbecue for 'Indirect heat' cooking, following the instructions on **page 14**.

Lightly rub the entire body of each duck with the butter. Place the ducks, head to tail, on a trivet (a cake rack will do) which has been set in a roasting tin. The tin should be of a size to sit comfortably on just one half of the barbecue's grill area if your unit is gas-fired. Apply several shots of Worcestershire sauce over each duck and then sprinkle with sufficient paprika to completely coat the birds' breasts and legs.

Cook, with medium to high heat, until the ducks are cooked to the desired degree. Depending on the weight of the individual ducks, and the way you like them cooked, this could take 25–75 minutes.

Remove the ducks and let them stand (or sit) for a few minutes. If they are large, cut them in half with poultry shears or heavy-duty kitchen scissors to double up the servings. Remove the trivet or rack from the roasting tin and carefully spoon off all the fat.

To make the gravy, blend the cornflour with the port and add to the tin juices. Place the tin over the barbecue's fire-bed and bring the gravy to the boil, stirring constantly. Boil and stir for a minute or so before spooning some of the rich sauce over the duck portions. Serve the remaining sauce in a separate bowl.

Christmas turkey

Cooking dinner on Christmas Day for a hungry gaggle of family and friends is quite a challenge – especially so when the poor old cook has to make do with rather limited cooking resources. However, for those families fortunate enough to possess a covered barbecue, a golden opportunity presents itself to give the cook, and particularly the member of the washing-up brigade who drew the short straw to clean the fat-splattered oven, a well-earned respite.

Barbecuing the turkey provides several major benefits:
1. Valuable oven space is freed for other pressing duties.
2. The turkey's succulence, taste, handsome appearance and aroma at least equals, if not surpasses, that of most oven-cooked birds and, if the turkey is smoke-cooked (a cooking technique that should only be practised in the great outdoors), its subsequent golden-mahogany veneer will further inflame the taste buds of the waiting company!
3. Neither rain nor snow will hinder your covered barbecue from carrying out its duty, although a cold wind whistling around the cooking area will result in a slightly extended cooking period and this should be factored into your timetable.
4. After the cook has braved the elements in order to retrieve the bird, he or she will be the recipient of appreciative backslapping from the expectant flock.

Prepare the barbecue for 'Indirect heat' cooking, following the instructions on **page 14**.

Ensure the giblets and neck have been removed from the turkey. Rinse the turkey all over, and inside its neck and body cavities, and pat dry with kitchen paper. Sprinkle the cavities generously with salt and pepper.

Tuck the wings behind the bird's back but leave the legs free, i.e. not tucked into the band of skin by the parson's nose, or tied closely together. Use your hand, or a brush, to spread groundnut oil, or softened butter or margarine, all over the bird. Lightly season the oiled surfaces with salt and freshly ground black pepper.

Position the turkey on the barbecue, partially shielding its lower sides with a narrow band of foil about 10cm (4 inches) wide. Tucking one edge of the foil band under the bird's back will help to secure it. Wrap a similar band of foil around each knuckle and lower part of the legs.

Cook the turkey over low/medium heat, with the lid down, until a meat thermometer registers 85°C (185°F) when positioned deep in the inside of the leg (make sure that the tip of the thermometer does not touch the bone and give a false reading).

The cooking time may vary considerably depending upon fuel type and quality, size of barbecue, weather conditions and of course the weight of the bird, but a 5–6 kg (11–13 lb) turkey should normally take around 2–2$\frac{1}{2}$ hours. Allow 20–30 minutes additional cooking time if the bird is fully stuffed at the neck. Roughly halfway through roasting the turkey, turn it 180 degrees to avoid uneven cooking.

The stuffing can be baked by placing it in 1 or 2 flameproof dishes fore and aft of the bird (not directly over the fire-bed) during the final 50–60 minutes of cooking.

The Finale:
Having given the waiting throng a brief glance at the golden bird to get their juices up and running, let the turkey rest for 20 minutes before carving.

Hickory-smoked turkey with a Scottish glaze

If you want to make your Christmas turkey look even more stunning, even more tasty, cook as in the previous recipe but add 2–3 chunks, or handfuls of small chips, of hickory wood (previously soaked in water) to the barbecue's fire-bed roughly halfway through the cooking period. Adding the wood earlier will intensify the bird's colour and its piquant flavour. During the final 15–20 minutes of cooking, brush the turkey all over with a glaze made by mixing about 50g (2oz) of softened butter with 2–3 tablespoons of Drambuie, or your favourite single malt whisky or liqueur.

Teriyaki turkey drumsticks

If you can't find small turkey drumsticks (they're often more akin in size to small legs of lamb), part-cook the larger drumsticks on the barbecue using the 'Indirect heat' method (see page 14) or in the kitchen oven, before finishing them on the grill.

Serves 6

6 small turkey drumsticks

For the marinade:
150ml (1/4 pint) soy sauce
4 tablespoons clear honey
3 tablespoons mirin or dry sherry
2 teaspoons freshly grated root ginger
150ml (1/4 pint) olive oil
2 garlic cloves, crushed
50g (2oz) spring onion, sliced thinly

Wash the drumsticks, pat dry with kitchen paper and pierce all over with the point of a skewer or sharp knife. Combine all the marinade ingredients and mix well. Pour over the drumsticks, turning them to make sure they are well coated. Cover the dish and leave in the refrigerator for a few hours or overnight. Turn the drumsticks occasionally while they are in the marinade.

Prepare the barbecue for grilling, following the instructions on **page 12**.

Briefly drain the drumsticks (reserve the marinade) and place on the grill. Cook over medium to high heat for about 40–50 minutes or until cooked, turning and basting frequently with the marinade. To check if they are cooked, pierce the thickest part with a skewer – the juices should run clear. If in doubt, cut the meat in the same area and check that it is no longer pink.

Spit-roasted saddle or loin of venison

Gooseberry or redcurrant jelly makes a delicious accompaniment to this handsome dish.

Serves 6–8

1.75–2.25kg (4–5 lb) saddle or loin of venison, trimmed of fat
125g (4oz) salt pork, cut into thin strips
2 garlic cloves, each cut into 4 slivers

For the basting sauce:
175g (6oz) clear honey
150ml (1/4 pint) soy sauce
300ml (1/2 pint) orange juice
juice of 1 lemon
150ml (1/4 pint) tomato ketchup
300ml (1/2 pint) red wine vinegar
1 teaspoon salt
1/2 teaspoon freshly ground black pepper
1 teaspoon mustard powder
1/2 teaspoon paprika

Prepare the barbecue for spit-roasting, following the instructions on **page 17**.

Wipe the venison with a damp cloth. Make slits in the meat and lard generously with the salt pork. Push the garlic slivers well down into the slits.

Combine all the marinade ingredients in a small pan and mix together over a low heat until blended.

Place the venison on the spit, balance it (see page 18) and secure firmly with the spit forks. Brush generously with the basting sauce and cook over medium heat if spit-roasting with the barbecue lid down, or over medium to high heat if using an open barbecue, until a meat thermometer inserted into the thickest part reads 60°C (140°F) for rare meat or 85°C (185°F) for well-done meat.

Allow the venison to stand for 10 minutes before carving.

Venison steaks with cranberry and red wine sauce

Serves 4–6

750g–1kg (1¹/₂–2 lb) loin of venison, boned and tied
salt pork or bacon fat, for larding (optional)
softened butter, for basting
1 tablespoon juniper berries, crushed

For the marinade:
250ml (8fl oz) dry red wine
1 medium onion, sliced
1 medium carrot, sliced
1 large bouquet garni
2 tablespoons olive oil
1 tablespoon red or white wine vinegar
6–8 black peppercorns

For the sauce:
2 tablespoons olive oil
2 shallots or 1 small onion, finely chopped
1 small carrot, finely chopped
¹/₂ celery stick, chopped
1 tablespoon plain flour
450ml (³/₄ pint) beef-bone stock
1 tablespoon cranberry jelly

Cut the venison into steaks (they will look similar to tournedos) 2.5–4cm (1–1¹/₂ inches) thick. Lard the steaks with salt pork or bacon fat, if desired.

To make the marinade, mix together the ingredients in a pan, bring to the boil and then leave until cold.

Place the steaks in a shallow dish and pour over the cold marinade. Cover the dish and leave for 6–8 hours or overnight in the refrigerator. Remove about 2 hours before cooking.

To prepare the sauce, heat the oil in a pan, add the shallots or onion, carrot and celery and cook until lightly coloured. Stir in the flour and cook slowly until the vegetables are nicely browned. Gradually stir in the stock and cook gently for about 30 minutes. Skim and strain the sauce. Then return it to the pan and continue simmering.

Prepare the barbecue for grilling, following the instructions on **page 12**.

Drain the steaks, reserving the marinade, and dry them with kitchen paper. Strain the marinade into the sauce and let it continue to simmer, skimming any scum from the surface. Add the cranberry jelly and continue simmering until the sauce is syrupy.

Meanwhile, sear the steaks over high heat for about 10 seconds on each side. Move the steaks to the sides of the grill. Reduce the heat to low/medium (if using a gas unit) or move the meat to a cooler spot on a charcoal unit, and continue grilling the steaks, basting frequently with softened butter, for a further 3–4 minutes on each side, adding the juniper berries as you turn the steaks, until cooked to the desired degree.

Spoon a little of the sauce over the steaks and serve immediately. Serve the remaining sauce separately.

pork

Pork & apple burgers; Pork & apricot kebabs; Indonesian pork satay with peanut sauce; Stir-fried pork with pineapple; Stir-fried pork with mushrooms & cabbage; Stir-fried pork with oyster sauce; Garlic & ginger spare ribs; Five-spice spare ribs; Spiced orange spare ribs; Smoked belly spare ribs with soy, orange & wine sauce; Spicy pork chops; Lemony pork chops; Hot and spicy pork steaks; Grilled gammon steaks with spicy apple sauce; Roast loin of pork with ambrosia stuffing; Soy-glazed roast loin of pork; Oriental pork belly; Spicy glazed baked ham; Caribbean pork rib roast; Baked ham with brown sugar glaze.

Pork & apple burgers

The flavours of pork and apple combine well to make this one of my favourite burgers.

Serves 6

1kg (2 lb) lean minced pork
1 medium apple, finely chopped
1 egg, beaten
75g (3oz) fresh white breadcrumbs
1 teaspoon garlic salt
1/4 teaspoon onion salt
1/4 teaspoon freshly ground black pepper
2 tablespoons olive oil
6 hamburger buns, halved

Prepare the barbecue for grilling, following the instructions on **page 12.**

Mix together the pork, apple, egg and enough of the breadcrumbs to give a firm, not too wet, mixture. Carefully shape into 6 burgers.

Blend together the garlic salt, onion salt, pepper and oil and brush some of the mixture on one side of the burgers.

Grill the oiled surfaces of the burgers, or cook on the griddle plate, over medium to high heat for about 10 minutes. Brush the burgers with the rest of the oil mixture, turn and cook on the other side for a further 10 minutes or until nicely browned.

Toast the buns during the last few minutes of cooking. Serve the burgers in the prepared buns with your favourite barbecue sauce (see pages 160–2).

Pork & apricot kebabs

Serves 4

8 shallots or 2 medium onions
oil for greasing metal skewers
500g (1 lb) pork tenderloin or boneless pork loin, cut into 2.5cm (1 inch) cubes
250g (8oz) can of apricot halves, drained
175g (6oz) soft brown sugar
4 tablespoons apricot jam
6 tablespoons red or white wine vinegar
3 tablespoons soy sauce
1 teaspoon mustard powder
salt and freshly ground black pepper

Prepare the barbecue for grilling, following the instructions on **page 12.**

If using shallots, parboil them for about 5 minutes; if using onions, parboil them whole for about 6–7 minutes and then cut into quarters.

Oil 4 metal skewers and thread the pork cubes, shallots or onion quarters and apricot halves onto them.

Combine the remaining ingredients in a small saucepan and heat gently until the sugar has dissolved. Brush the kebabs all over with the mixture. Place them on the grill and cook over medium heat for about 15 minutes. Turn and baste the kebabs several times during cooking.

 Note: Pineapple chunks may be used instead of the apricot halves. In which case, replace the apricot jam with marmalade and half the wine vinegar with the same quantity of pineapple juice.

Indonesian pork satay with peanut sauce

Serves 4

3 tablespoons soy sauce
3 tablespoons groundnut oil, plus extra for basting
1 tablespoon chopped onion
1 garlic clove, crushed
1 teaspoon sugar
a pinch of mild curry powder
1.1kg (2^1/$_2$ lb) boneless pork loin,
cut into 2.5 x 10 x 0.5cm (1 x 4 x ^{1}/$_4$ inch) strips

For the peanut sauce:
50g (2oz) shredded coconut flesh
150ml (^{1}/$_4$ pint) hot milk
2 tablespoons softened butter
^{1}/$_2$ teaspoon mild curry powder
^{1}/$_2$ teaspoon freshly grated root ginger
1 garlic clove, very finely chopped
1 medium onion, finely chopped
50g (2oz) crushed pineapple
150ml (^{1}/$_4$ pint) chicken stock
2 tablespoons sugar
3 tablespoons smooth peanut butter
^{1}/$_2$ teaspoon salt
a pinch of freshly ground black pepper

Combine the soy sauce, oil, onion, garlic, sugar and curry powder in a bowl. Marinate the pork strips in the mixture, in the refrigerator, for 2–3 hours, stirring occasionally.

Meanwhile, make the peanut sauce. Soak the coconut in the milk for about 30 minutes. Then melt the butter in a flameproof dish or deep frying pan, add the curry powder and cook, over fairly gentle heat, for 1 minute. Add the ginger, garlic and onion and continue to cook for 5 minutes. Add the soaked coconut and milk, pineapple, chicken stock, sugar and peanut butter. Season with the salt and pepper and cook for 15–20 minutes, stirring occasionally.

Soak 12 bamboo skewers in water, and prepare the barbecue for grilling, following the instructions on **page 12.**

Drain the meat and thread onto the bamboo skewers (you can use oiled metal ones if you wish). Cook over medium to high heat for 5–10 minutes. Turn and baste frequently with groundnut oil. Serve the pork skewers with the peanut sauce.

Stir-fried pork with pineapple

Serves 4

500g (1 lb) lean pork, preferably tenderloin,
cut into thin strips
4 tablespoons vegetable oil
1 large onion, coarsely chopped
1 green pepper, de-seeded and cut into
2cm (³/4 inch) squares
1 teaspoon finely grated fresh root ginger
3 tablespoons soy sauce
1 tablespoon dry sherry or sake
1 tablespoon red wine vinegar
¹/4 teaspoon salt
¹/2 teaspoon sugar
250g (8oz) can of pineapple chunks, with the
juice reserved
250g (8oz) can of water chestnuts, drained
and sliced
2 level tablespoons cornflour, blended
with 3 tablespoons cold water

Prepare the barbecue for wok-cooking, following the instructions on **page 19**.

Stir-fry the pork in 2 tablespoons of the oil over high heat for about 5 minutes. Remove from the wok and put to one side of the grill. Add the remaining oil to the wok and stir-fry the onion and pepper for about 2 minutes. Return the pork to the wok and stir in the ginger, soy sauce, sherry or sake, vinegar, salt and sugar. Add the pineapple chunks and make up the reserved juice to 300ml (¹/2 pint) with water. Add the diluted juice to the wok along with the water chestnuts. Stir in the blended cornflour and stir-fry for 2–3 minutes.

Stir-fried pork with mushrooms & cabbage

Stir-frying can be likened to a dance – slow, quick, quick, slow. The first step in the dance is the patient preparation that needs to be carried out before heating the wok. Stir-frying the prepared food constitutes the quick steps. This high-speed action demands that the prepared food, cooking implements and serving dishes are easily to hand. The final slow step is when you sit down to savour and enjoy the food.

Serves 4

750g (1¹/2 lb) lean pork, thinly sliced
into bite-sized pieces
1 teaspoon salt
1 tablespoon cornflour
3 tablespoons vegetable oil
500g (1 lb) spring cabbage
3 tablespoons lard
250g (8oz) open-cap mushrooms, halved,
or sliced and stalks discarded
1¹/2 tablespoons soy sauce
3 tablespoons chicken stock
¹/2 teaspoon sesame oil
2 teaspoons sugar

Prepare the barbecue for wok-cooking, following the instructions on **page 19**.

Sprinkle the pork pieces with the salt, cornflour and 1 tablespoon of the vegetable oil and mix together lightly. Remove the tougher stems from the cabbage and cut the leaves into 5cm (2 inch) pieces.

Position the wok on the barbecue and melt the lard. When hot, add the mushrooms and cabbage. Stir-fry over high heat for 2 minutes. Add the soy sauce and chicken stock and continue to stir-fry for 1 minute. Cover the wok and cook over medium heat for a further 2 minutes. Turn out the vegetables onto a warmed dish and cover. Pour the remaining vegetable oil into the wok and, when hot, add the pork and stir-fry over high heat for 2–3 minutes. Add the sesame oil and sugar and stir-fry for a further 2 minutes. Return the vegetables to the pork and continue stir-frying for 1 minute. Serve immediately, with rice or noodles if liked.

Stir-fried pork with oyster sauce

Serves 4

250g (8oz) lean pork, preferably tenderloin,
sliced into bite-size pieces
250g (8oz) spinach
3 tablespoons vegetable oil
$1/2$ teaspoon salt
$1/4$ teaspoon sugar
2 tablespoons oyster sauce
6 baby sweetcorn, broken into small pieces
$1/2$ teaspoon sesame oil
freshly ground black pepper

For the marinade:
$1/2$ teaspoon soy sauce
$1/2$ teaspoon sesame oil
1 teaspoon rice wine or dry sherry
$1/2$ teaspoon sugar
1 egg yolk
1 tablespoon cornflour
salt and freshly ground black pepper

Prepare the barbecue for wok-cooking, following the instructions on **page 19**.

For the marinade, combine the soy sauce, sesame oil, rice wine or sherry, sugar, egg yolk and salt and pepper to taste and mix well. Stir the pork into this mixture and marinate for about 10 minutes. Stir in the cornflour just before cooking.

Cut the spinach into 5cm (2 inch) pieces. Position the wok on the barbecue and heat 1 tablespoon of the vegetable oil. Add the salt and the spinach and stir-fry quickly over high heat. Add the sugar and 1 tablespoon water and stir again. Drain the liquid from the wok, remove the spinach and keep warm.

Heat the remaining vegetable oil in the wok and stir-fry the pork over high heat until golden brown all over. Remove the pork from the wok and keep warm. Add the oyster sauce to the wok and when the liquid begins to bubble, return the pork pieces to it and stir-fry for about a minute. Return the spinach and add the sweetcorn. Sprinkle with the sesame oil and pepper to taste, and stir for another minute or so. Serve immediately.

Garlic & ginger spare ribs

Serves around 6

2.75kg (6 lb) lean spare ribs

For the marinade:
4 garlic cloves, very finely chopped
2 tablespoons preserved ginger, finely chopped
275ml (9fl oz) chicken stock
125g (4oz) orange marmalade
3 tablespoons red wine vinegar
3 tablespoons tomato ketchup
2 teaspoons soy sauce

Mix all the marinade ingredients together.

If the ribs are in whole slabs, cut into 3 or 4 rib sections. Place the ribs, together with the marinade, in a strong plastic bag and securely close the bag with a twist-tie. Put the bag in a roasting tin or large dish (in case of leakage) and refrigerate for 12–24 hours, turning the bag occasionally.

Prepare the barbecue for grilling, following the instructions on **page 12**.

Remove the ribs from the marinade and drain briefly, reserving the marinade. Cook over medium heat for about 1$\frac{1}{4}$ hours or until the meat pulls away from the rib ends exposing 1–2cm ($\frac{1}{2}$–$\frac{3}{4}$ inch) of bone.

Turn the ribs frequently but baste only occasionally, and not too liberally, with the reserved marinade.

 Serve immediately, accompanied, I suggest, by boiled rice.

Five-spice spare ribs

The rich, delicious blend of Chinese five-spice powder and sumptuous sauces in this recipe will ensure that there will be no spare, spare ribs left over from the cookout … only some bones in remarkably pristine condition!

Serves 2–4

1.25kg (3 lb) meaty spare ribs

For the marinade:
1 tablespoon rice wine or dry sherry
1 tablespoon oyster sauce
4 tablespoons hoisin sauce
50g (2oz) sugar
$\frac{1}{2}$ teaspoon five-spice powder

Mix all the marinade ingredients together.

If the ribs are in whole slabs, cut into 3 or 4 rib sections. Place the ribs, together with the marinade, in a strong plastic bag and securely close the bag with a twist-tie. Put the bag in a roasting tin or large dish (in case of leakage) and refrigerate for 12–24 hours, turning the bag occasionally.

Prepare the barbecue for grilling, following the instructions on **page 12**.

Remove the ribs from the marinade and drain briefly, reserving the marinade. Cook the ribs, over medium heat, for about 1$\frac{1}{4}$ hours or until the meat has pulled away from the rib ends exposing 1–2cm ($\frac{1}{2}$–$\frac{3}{4}$ inch) of bone.

Turn the ribs frequently, basting 2 or 3 times with the reserved marinade during the final 10–15 minutes of cooking. Serve with a roll of kitchen paper!

Spiced orange spare ribs

Orange juice, lemon juice, Worcestershire sauce and honey combine to give the ribs a delicious sweet spicy flavour while, at the same time, imparting a handsome glaze.

Serves 2–4

1.25kg (3 lb) lean spare ribs

For the marinade:
2 tablespoons clear honey
juice of $1/2$ lemon
grated zest of $1/2$ orange and
juice of 2 oranges
2 tablespoons Worcestershire sauce
2 teaspoons soy sauce
salt

Mix together the marinade ingredients in a pan and heat gently. Simmer for 2 minutes and allow to cool.

If the ribs are in whole slabs, cut into 3 or 4 rib sections. Place the ribs, together with the marinade, in a strong plastic bag and securely close the bag with a twist-tie. Put the bag in a roasting tin or large dish (in case of leakage) and refrigerate for 12–24 hours, turning the bag occasionally.

Prepare the barbecue for grilling, following the instructions on **page 12**.

Remove the ribs from the marinade and drain briefly, reserving the marinade. Cook the ribs over medium heat for about $11/4$ hours or until the meat has pulled away from the rib ends exposing 1–2cm ($1/2$–$3/4$ inch) of bone. If the ribs are 'mean on meat', the cooking time can be reduced.

Turn the ribs frequently during the cooking time, but baste occasionally only during the final 15 minutes, so that the surface of the ribs doesn't become charred. When cooked through the spare ribs will have a deep golden, semi-translucent appearance and the meat will be tender and juicy.

Smoked belly spare ribs with soy, orange & wine sauce

Simply delicious, full of flavour and with a lingering, nose-twitching aroma. If you are buying a rack of ribs, rather than a bag of pre-cut ones (which are often very different in terms of size and meat to bone ratio), slice the rack into separate ribs by cutting as close as possible to the right-hand bone. This will provide a thicker covering of succulent meat to nibble away at.

Serves 4

1 quantity Soy, orange and wine sauce (see page 162)
12 lean pork-belly spare ribs
1 hickory chunk or 1 handful of small
hickory chips (previously soaked in water)

Make the soy, orange and wine sauce.

Prepare the barbecue for 'Indirect heat' cooking, following the instructions on **page 14**. Add the dampened hickory to the charcoal or gas fire-bed.

Place the ribs on the centre of the grill with the fat facing the fire-bed. Cook with the lid on, over medium/high heat, for 25–30 minutes, basting the ribs occasionally with half the soy orange and wine sauce.

Serve the ribs with the remaining sauce.

Spicy pork chops

The delicious spicy flavour and attractive appearance, comes from a combination of Dijon mustard, soy sauce, chilli powder and honey.

Serves 6

6 pork loin chops, 2.5cm (1 inch) thick

For the marinade:
6 tablespoons clear honey
6 tablespoons Dijon mustard
2 tablespoons soy sauce
$1/4$ teaspoon chilli powder
$1/2$ teaspoon salt

Pat the chops dry with kitchen paper and slash the fat around the edge of each at 1cm ($1/2$ inch) intervals.

Combine the marinade ingredients.

Place the chops in a shallow dish and spoon the marinade over the meat. Cover and refrigerate for 6–24 hours, turning the chops once or twice.

Prepare the barbecue for grilling, following the instructions on **page 12**.

Remove the chops from the marinade and drain briefly, reserving the marinade. Place on the grill. Cook over medium to high heat for 15–20 minutes on each side or until any pinkness in the centre of the meat has disappeared. Baste the chops with the marinade just before turning and during the final few minutes of cooking.

Lemony pork chops

Serves 4

4 loin or chump chops, cut 2.5cm (1 inch) thick

For the marinade:
juice and grated zest of 1 lemon
4 bay leaves
4 tablespoons olive oil
1 tablespoon chopped fresh parsley
a pinch of dried oregano
a pinch of dried thyme
a pinch of dried sage
a pinch of salt
$1/4$ teaspoon freshly ground black pepper
1 garlic clove, crushed

Pat the chops dry with kitchen paper and slash the fat around the edge of each at 1cm ($1/2$ inch) intervals.

Combine the marinade ingredients.

Place the chops in a shallow dish and spoon the marinade over the meat. Cover and refrigerate for 6–24 hours, turning the chops once or twice.

Prepare the barbecue for grilling, following the instructions on **page 12**.

Remove the chops from the marinade and drain briefly, reserving the marinade. Place on the grill. Cook over medium to high heat for 15–20 minutes on each side or until any pinkness in the centre of the meat has disappeared. Baste the chops occasionally with the marinade during cooking.

Hot & spicy pork steaks

Serves 4

4 pork shoulder steaks

For the marinade:
2 teaspoons wholegrain mustard
1 teaspoon paprika
1 garlic clove, crushed
1 fresh green chilli, finely chopped
2–3 drops Tabasco
4 tablespoons white wine vinegar
4 tablespoons olive oil
salt and freshly ground black pepper

Combine the marinade ingredients. Place the pork steaks in a shallow dish and spoon the marinade over them. Cover and leave to marinate for 2 hours.

Prepare the barbecue for grilling, following the instructions on **page 12**.

Remove the steaks from the marinade and drain briefly, reserving the marinade. Place on the grill. Cook over medium to high heat for 15–20 minutes or until any pinkness in the centre of the meat has disappeared. Baste the steaks with the reserved marinade during the final few minutes of cooking.

Grilled gammon steaks with spicy apple sauce

Serves 4

3 tablespoons good-quality, shop-bought apple sauce
2 tablespoons orange juice
1 teaspoon grated orange zest
2 teaspoons Dijon mustard
a pinch of dried thyme
a pinch of dried sage
4 gammon steaks

Prepare the barbecue for grilling, following the instructions on **page 12**.

Mix together the apple sauce, orange juice and zest, and stir in the mustard, thyme and sage.

Brush the apple mixture over one side of the gammon steaks. Grill the coated side over medium heat for about 3 minutes.

Brush the tops of the steaks with more apple mixture, turn them over and grill for a further 3 minutes. Continue brushing and turning the steaks until done. Serve immediately, with some additional apple sauce and mustard.

Roast loin of pork
with ambrosia stuffing

Serves 6–8

1.75kg (4 lb) loin of pork, boned and rolled

For the ambrosia stuffing:
3 tablespoons softened butter, plus
3 tablespoons melted butter
2 medium onions, chopped
2 medium cooking or eating apples, cored,
peeled and chopped
175g (6oz) green olives, stoned and chopped
75g (3oz) walnuts, chopped
1/4 teaspoon dried thyme
1/2 teaspoon salt
75g (3oz) fresh white breadcrumbs
75g (3oz) cooked ham, chopped

Prepare the barbecue for 'Indirect heat' cooking, following the instructions on **page 14**.

Using a sharp knife, slice halfway through the loin at 2.5cm (1 inch) intervals. Then cut further down into each incision to form deep pockets, taking care to leave a 2.5cm (1 inch) wall on the sides and bottom of the loin.

To make the stuffing, heat the softened butter in a skillet or frying pan and cook the onions, stirring occasionally, until transparent. Add the apples and continue cooking for 1 minute. Add the olives, walnuts, thyme, salt, breadcrumbs, melted butter and ham and mix well.

Fill each pocket in the loin generously with the stuffing. Tie the roll lengthways at 2.5cm (1 inch) intervals to hold it firmly together.

Roast over medium to high heat for about 1 1/2–2 hours until the meat is well done. A meat thermometer buried in the centre of the roast should register 85°C (185°F).

Remove the roast from the barbecue and allow to stand for about 10 minutes before carving. Remove the string and slice through the meat between the pockets to make individually stuffed portions.

Soy-glazed roast loin of pork

The combination of soy sauce, apple juice, garlic and ginger on the skin of the loin produces a dark and handsome glaze. For those who like the crisp, tasty crackling, serve the meat with a strip or two, and an extra napkin. This dish is equally delicious when served hot or cold.

Serves 6–8

125ml (4fl oz) apple juice
3 tablespoons soy sauce
1 garlic clove, very finely chopped
1 teaspoon freshly grated root ginger
1.75kg (4 lb) loin of pork,
boned and rolled
2 spring onions, finely sliced,
to garnish (optional)

Prepare the barbecue for 'Indirect heat' cooking, following the instructions on **page 14**. (Use a drip pan.)

Mix together the apple juice, soy sauce, garlic and ginger and place on one side.

With a sharp, short-bladed knife e.g. a Stanley knife, score the skin of the loin at roughly 1cm ($1/2$ inch) intervals.

Roast the loin, fat side up, with medium heat, for 1 hour. Generously baste the scored skin with the soy sauce mixture. Cook the loin for a further $1^{1}/_{2}$ hours or until the meat is well done (a meat thermometer inserted into the thickest part should register 85°C/185°F). Baste frequently during the final 20–30 minutes of cooking to produce an attractive dark glaze. Slice and serve, garnished with spring onion, if using.

The juices collected in the drip pan will make a rich and very tasty gravy.

Oriental pork belly

Spicy glazed baked ham

Oriental pork belly tastes yummy hot or cold and goes well with jacket potatoes.

Serves 6–8

1.25kg (3 lb) belly of pork on the bone

For the marinade:
1 garlic clove
1/2 teaspoon salt
3 tablespoons soy sauce
4 tablespoons clear honey
1/2 teaspoon ground cinnamon

Using a sharp knife, carefully remove the rind from the pork, leaving the fat intact. Score the fat to leave a diamond pattern.

Crush the garlic and salt together in a pestle and mortar. Mix with the soy sauce, honey and cinnamon in a shallow dish.

Place the pork skin side down in the marinade. Cover the dish and refrigerate for 6–24 hours. Remove the dish from the refrigerator an hour or so before cooking to allow the meat to reach room temperature.

Prepare the barbecue for 'Indirect heat' cooking, following the instructions on **page 14**.

Half-fill a roasting tin with hot water and cover with a wire rack. Place the roasting tin on the unlit side of the barbecue.

Remove the pork from the marinade, reserving the marinade. Place, skin side down, in the centre of the wire rack. Cook with medium heat for 1 hour. Turn the meat over and baste with the reserved marinade. Cook for a further hour.

Cut the pork into thin slices, down to the bone, before serving.

Serves 25–30

5–6kg (12–14 lb) boneless cooked gammon
4 tablespoons oyster sauce
2 tablespoons dry sherry
2–3 tablespoons whole cloves

Prepare the barbecue for 'Indirect heat' cooking, following the instructions on **page 14**.

Using a sharp knife, cut through the rind (to the fat) down the middle of the gammon and around its circumference. Position the ham on the barbecue and cook at medium heat for 30–40 minutes or until the rind down the middle moves apart by 2.5cm (1 inch) or so. Pull the rind away from the ham and score the fat in a diamond pattern.

Combine the oyster sauce and sherry.

Rub the scored surface of the ham with the mixture and stick a single clove into the centre of each diamond. Continue cooking, with the lid down, at medium heat, for a further 2 hours or so or until a meat thermometer registers 85°C (185°F). If you do not have a meat thermometer allow 8–10 minutes per 500g (1 lb). Avoid cooking the ham at too high a temperature.

 Note: As an alternative to the above glaze, try using orange marmalade or a mixture of soft brown sugar, mustard powder and pineapple syrup.

Caribbean pork rib roast

Serves 3–4

1–1.25kg (2–3 lb) pork rib
1 tablespoon dark rum

For the Caribbean rub:
1 tablespoon soft brown sugar
2 teaspoons ground allspice
2 teaspoons onion powder
$1/2$ teaspoon dried thyme
1 teaspoon salt
$1/2$ teaspoon ground nutmeg

For the mango sauce:
1 mango, peeled and chopped
$1/2$ medium onion, chopped
2 tablespoons mango chutney
125ml (4fl oz) chicken stock
2–3 tablespoons dark rum
2 tablespoons cream of coconut
1 teaspoon Caribbean rub (see above)
25g (1oz) butter
salt and freshly ground black pepper

The night before you plan to barbecue, combine the Caribbean rub ingredients in a small bowl. Massage the pork well with the rum and then with about half the rub. Transfer the pork to a plastic bag, or wrap it in cling film, and refrigerate overnight.

Prepare the barbecue for 'Indirect heat' cooking, following the instructions on **page 14**.

Remove the pork from the refrigerator and pat it lightly with another coating of rub. Let the meat sit at room temperature for 30–40 minutes before transferring it to the barbecue, fattier side up. Cook for $4^1/2$–5 hours at a low temperature of 60–70°C (140–160°F).

While the roast cooks, prepare the mango sauce. In a food processor or blender, purée together the mango, onion and chutney, pouring in some of the chicken stock if the mixture is a little thick. Spoon the mixture into a heavy-based saucepan and add the remaining stock, rum, cream of coconut and Caribbean rub. Warm over a medium heat and simmer for about 20 minutes. Taste, and add as much salt and pepper as necessary to balance the savoury and sweet flavours. The sauce can be kept warm, or refrigerated and then re-heated when the meat is ready. The butter should be added to the warm sauce just before serving.

After removing the pork from the barbecue, allow it to sit at room temperature for 10–15 minutes before carving. Serve with the warm mango sauce.

Baked ham with brown sugar glaze

Serves 8–10

2.25kg (5 lb) piece of middle cut gammon, rolled
750ml (1¹/₂ pints) dry cider
1 medium onion, stuck with 6–10 cloves
2 bay leaves
6 black peppercorns
about 36 cloves

For the brown sugar glaze:
125g (4oz) soft brown sugar
¹/₂ teaspoon ground cinnamon
1 tablespoon English mustard
4 tablespoons beer or cider, or cranberry, apple or orange juice

Soak the gammon in cold water for a few hours (change the water during this period). Remove the joint and place in a saucepan or casserole that will accommodate it comfortably.

Pour over 600ml (1 pint) of the cider plus enough cold water to cover the gammon completely. Add the onion, bay leaves and peppercorns, bring to the boil and simmer gently for 1 hour.

Drain the gammon, let it cool a little, remove the string and carefully cut off the skin. Stand the gammon, fat side uppermost, in a roasting tin. Pour the remainder of the cider into the tin. Lightly score the fat in diagonal lines (about 2.5cm/1 inch apart) in different directions to form diamond shapes.

Prepare the barbecue for 'Indirect heat' cooking, following the instructions on **page 14**.

Combine the ingredients for the glaze in a small saucepan and heat gently until the sugar has dissolved. Brush the glaze mixture all over the gammon. Insert a clove in the centre of each diamond shape.

Bake the gammon, with medium heat, for 1–1¹/₄ hours, basting occasionally with the cider-enriched juices.

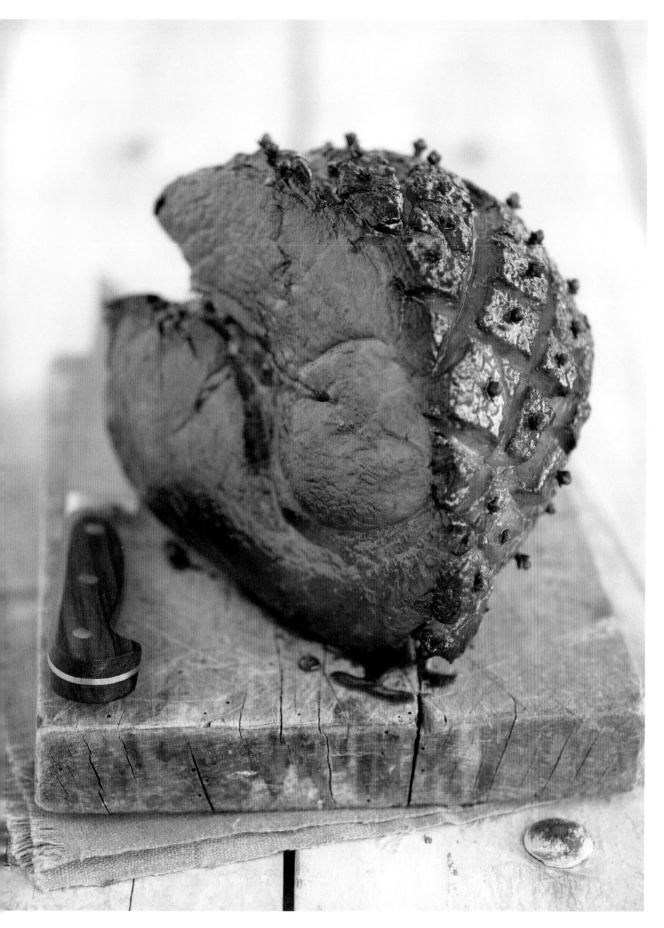

lamb

Lambapple burgers; Angela's heavenly minty lamb kebabs; Turkistan kebabs; Lamb satay; Greek lamb kebabs; Andalusian lamb chops; Orange, mint & ginger double lamb loin chops; Cinnamon lamb cutlets; Soy & ginger-flavoured lamb cutlets; Lemony lamb leg steaks; Harry's heavenly herb & honey roast lamb; Lamb noisettes with cheese; Mint jelly glazed breast of lamb; Spit-roasted chilli-stuffed leg of lamb; Sweet & sour shoulder of lamb; Butterflied leg of lamb in a herb crust; Crown of roast lamb; Spit-roasted leg of lamb with anchovies, garlic & rosemary; Lamb's kidney brochettes with sauce Bercy; Herb-stuffed lamb's kidneys; Caul-wrapped marinated lamb's liver.

Lambapple burgers

Serves 6

500g (1 lb) minced lamb
2 tablespoons chopped fresh parsley
a generous pinch of dried rosemary
2 teaspoons soy sauce
$1/4$ teaspoon salt
a pinch of freshly ground pepper
275g (9oz) can of pineapple slices
50g (2oz) soft brown sugar
2 teaspoons Worcestershire sauce
6 tablespoons tomato ketchup

Prepare the barbecue for grilling, following the instructions on **page 12**.

Place the minced lamb, herbs, soy sauce and salt and pepper in a bowl and mix together. Lightly press the mixture into 6 burger shapes. Drain the pineapple slices and reserve about 2 tablespoons of the juice.

Press a pineapple slice into the surface of each burger and mould the minced meat up and around the edge of the pineapple slice.

Place the sugar, Worcestershire sauce, tomato ketchup and reserved pineapple juice in a pan and heat gently for a few minutes, stirring occasionally.

Brush the warmed sauce over the burgers and grill, or cook on the griddle plate, over medium to high heat, for about 10 minutes or until the meat is cooked. Baste frequently with the sauce to glaze the pineapple slices, and close the barbecue lid for the final 2 minutes or so of cooking to enhance the glaze.

Angela's heavenly minty lamb kebabs

Serves 4

750g ($1^1/2$ lb) lean boneless lamb,
cut into 2.5cm (1 inch) cubes
oil for greasing skewers

For the marinade:
150g (5oz) carton natural yoghurt
1 tablespoon olive oil
1 teaspoon mint sauce
$1/2$ teaspoon freshly grated root ginger
or $1/4$ teaspoon ground ginger
salt and freshly ground black pepper

Mix all the marinade ingredients together. Add the lamb and leave in a cool place to marinate for at least 3–4 hours.

Prepare the barbecue for grilling, following the instructions on **page 12**.

Drain the lamb, reserving the marinade, and thread onto 4 oiled metal skewers, leaving a small gap between each cube.

Place the kebabs on the grill or griddle plate and cook over medium heat for about 10–15 minutes, depending upon how well done you like your lamb. Turn the kebabs several times during cooking, basting occasionally with the reserved marinade. Serve with Brown rice and vegetable salad (see page 131) if liked.

Turkistan kebabs

Centuries ago, the fierce Turkish warriors used their swords to impale pieces of meat for grilling over the camp fire. Thus, so it is believed, began the art of skewer cooking.

Serves 6

1kg (2 lb) lean boneless lamb
175g (6oz) suet
125g (4oz) onion, finely chopped
25g (1oz) fresh parsley, finely chopped
1 garlic clove, very finely chopped
1 teaspoon paprika
1/2 teaspoon freshly ground black pepper
2 teaspoons salt
2 teaspoon lemon juice
2 eggs
oil for greasing skewers and brushing

Pass the lamb and suet through the medium-size disc of a grinder. Combine this mixture with the onion, parsley, garlic, paprika, pepper, salt and lemon juice and pass through the grinder – this time fitted with the fine disc – again. Blend thoroughly. Add the eggs and, with wet hands, mix well. Chill the mixture in the refrigerator for about 30 minutes or until firm.

Prepare the barbecue for grilling, following the instructions on **page 12**.

Re-wet your hands and mould the meat mixture onto 6 oiled skewers to form torpedo-shaped kebabs about 7.5cm (3 inches) long and 2.5cm (1 inch) in diameter.

Brush the kebabs with oil and grill over high heat for 8–10 minutes, turning to brown on all sides. These are great served with **Pilau rice** (page 128).

Lamb satay

Serves 6

1kg (2 lb) fillet end leg of lamb
oil for greasing skewers

For the marinade:
4 tablespoons soy sauce
3 garlic cloves, crushed
1 small onion, finely chopped
1 tablespoon lemon juice
1 tablespoon soft brown sugar

For the satay sauce:
2 teaspoons groundnut oil
1 large garlic clove, crushed
3 tablespoons smooth peanut butter
1^1/$_2$ tablespoons soy sauce
2 teaspoons lemon juice
1 green or red chilli, de-seeded and
finely chopped
50g (2oz) creamed coconut
3 tablespoons chicken stock

Cut the lamb into 2.5cm (1 inch) cubes, removing any fat or gristle. Mix together the ingredients for the marinade in a large bowl. Add the cubes of meat and turn to coat evenly with the marinade. Cover the bowl and leave at room temperature for about an hour.

Prepare the barbecue for grilling, following the instructions on **page 12**.

Meanwhile, prepare the sauce. Heat the oil in a saucepan and cook the garlic over low heat for 1–2 minutes. Add the peanut butter and cook, stirring, until it starts to darken. Add the soy sauce, lemon juice, chilli, creamed coconut and chicken stock and bring slowly to the boil, stirring constantly. Remove the pan to a corner of the grill, or place on the warming grill, and simmer for 5–6 minutes, stirring occasionally. Keep the sauce warm.

Lightly drain the lamb cubes, discarding the marinade, and thread them onto 6 oiled metal skewers, leaving a small gap between the cubes. Cook over high heat for 10–15 minutes until browned on all sides.

Pour the prepared sauce into individual warmed dishes and serve immediately with the lamb.

Greek lamb kebabs

Serves 4

750g (1¹/₂ lb) lamb leg steaks
1 teaspoon dried marjoram or 1 tablespoon chopped fresh marjoram
2 small onions, peeled and quartered
4 tablespoons olive oil, plus extra for greasing skewers
1 tablespoon lemon juice
8 bay leaves
salt and freshly ground black pepper

Trim the lamb, and cut into 2cm (³/₄ inch) cubes. Place the cubes in a dish and season with salt, pepper and marjoram. Break the onions into layers and add the thick outer layers to the dish. Reserve the inner layers. Add the oil and lemon juice, stir well and cover the dish with cling film. Leave in a cool place to marinate for 3–4 hours.

Prepare the barbecue for grilling, following the instructions on **page 12**.

Divide the cubes of lamb between 4 oiled metal skewers, impaling an onion layer and half a bay leaf between every 2 pieces of meat.

Place the kebabs on the grill and cook over medium heat for about 10–15 minutes, depending upon how well done you like your lamb. Turn the kebabs several times during cooking.

Serve with a plain tomato salad and a garnish of lemon wedges.

Andalusian lamb chops

Serves 6

6 lamb chump chops

For the marinade:
2 tablespoons finely chopped onion
150ml (¹/₄ pint) dry sherry
1 bay leaf
¹/₂ teaspoon dried oregano
1 teaspoon dried basil
3 tablespoons tarragon vinegar
6 tablespoons olive oil
¹/₂ teaspoon freshly ground black pepper

Place the chops in a shallow dish. Mix together the marinade ingredients and pour over the meat. Cover and marinate overnight in the refrigerator, or for 4–6 hours at room temperature, turning the chops occasionally.

If refrigerated, allow the meat to stand at room temperature for about an hour before cooking.

Prepare the barbecue for grilling, following the instructions on **page 12**.

Lightly drain the chops and reserve the marinade. Place the chops on the grill and cook over medium to high heat for about 10–12 minutes on each side, basting occasionally with the reserved marinade.

Orange, mint & ginger double lamb loin chops

Cinnamon lamb cutlets

The orange, mint and ginger marinade gives the lamb a fresh, slightly sharp, flavour.

Serves 4

4 x 2–2.5cm (3/4–1 inch) thick lamb double loin chops
1 tablespoon chopped fresh parsley, to garnish

For the marinade:
grated zest and juice of 1 large orange
3 tablespoons chopped fresh mint
1 teaspoon freshly grated root ginger

Place the chops in a shallow dish large enough for them to be accommodated side by side.

Mix together the ingredients for the marinade and pour over the meat. Turn the chops twice to coat well. Cover the dish with cling film and leave for at least 3 hours at room temperature or overnight in the refrigerator. If refrigerated, allow the meat to stand at room temperature for 2–3 hours before cooking.

Prepare the barbecue for grilling, following the instructions on **page 12**.

Remove the chops from the marinade and drain briefly. Place the chops on the grill, over medium to high heat, and cook for 6–7 minutes on each side, or until done to your liking.

Scatter over the parsley before serving.

Serves 6

12 lamb cutlets

For the marinade:
$1^1/_2$ teaspoons ground cinnamon
1 tablespoon soft brown sugar
3 tablespoons olive oil
6 tablespoons orange juice
$^1/_4$ teaspoon freshly ground black pepper
$^1/_4$ teaspoon salt

Place the cutlets in a shallow dish. Mix together the marinade ingredients. Pour the marinade over the meat, turning it once or twice so the cutlets are well coated. Cover and marinate at room temperature for about 4 hours, or overnight in a refrigerator, turning the cutlets twice during this period.

Prepare the barbecue for grilling, following the instructions on **page 12**.

Briefly drain the cutlets and reserve the marinade. Place the cutlets on the grill and cook over medium heat for about 25 minutes, turning and basting occasionally with the reserved marinade.

Soy & ginger-flavoured lamb cutlets

Teriyaki marinade is widely available from stores and supermarkets, or you can make your own following the recipe on page 158 (in which case you will have to omit the honey). The marinade in this recipe can also be used for chicken and pork.

Serves 6

12 lamb cutlets

For the marinade:
3 tablespoons groundnut oil
$1^1/_2$ tablespoons Teriyaki marinade
1 tablespoon sake or white wine vinegar
1 tablespoon wholegrain Dijon mustard
1 small piece of fresh root ginger, peeled and grated

Place the cutlets in a shallow dish. Mix together the marinade ingredients and pour over the meat. Turn the meat once or twice so that it is evenly coated. Marinate at room temperature for about 2 hours, turning the cutlets twice.

Prepare the barbecue for grilling, following the instructions on **page 12**.

Briefly drain the cutlets and reserve the marinade. Place on the grill and cook over medium heat for about 15 minutes, turning and basting occasionally with the reserved marinade.

Lemony lamb leg steaks

Serves 4

4 x 2–2.5cm ($^3/_4$–1 inch) thick lamb leg steaks
1 lemon, sliced, to garnish

For the marinade:
150ml ($^1/_4$ pint) oil
6 tablespoons lemon juice
1 teaspoon salt
1 teaspoon dried oregano
1 medium onion, finely chopped
1 garlic clove, crushed
$^1/_4$ teaspoon freshly ground black pepper

Place the leg steaks in a shallow dish. Mix together the ingredients for the marinade and pour over the meat. Turn the meat twice to coat well. Cover the dish and leave for at least 4 hours at room temperature, or overnight in the refrigerator. If refrigerated, allow the meat to stand at room temperature for 2–3 hours before cooking.

Prepare the barbecue for grilling, following the instructions on **page 12**.

Remove the steaks from the marinade and drain briefly. Cook over medium to high heat for 6–7 minutes on each side, or until done to your liking. Garnish with the lemon slices before serving.

Harry's heavenly herb & honey roast lamb

Serves 6–8

2 racks of lamb, chined
3 tablespoons clear honey, warmed
2 tablespoons chopped fresh mixed herbs
(e.g. mint, rosemary, thyme, marjoram or tarragon)
5 tablespoons fresh white breadcrumbs
2 teaspoons grated lemon zest
salt and freshly ground black pepper

With a sharp, short-bladed knife carefully trim the meat and fat 2.5cm (1 inch) from the end of the rib bones on each joint.

Prepare the barbecue for 'Indirect heat' cooking, following the instructions on **page 14**.

Brush the surface of the lamb with the warm honey. Mix together the herbs, breadcrumbs, lemon zest, salt and pepper. Sprinkle the mixture evenly over the surface of the fat.

Cook with medium heat for about 1^1/$_4$ hours or until cooked to the desired degree. To serve, carve between the rib bones to yield 7–8 slices per rack.

Lamb noisettes with cheese

Serves 6

6 lamb noisettes, about 2.5cm (1 inch) thick
175g (6oz) blue cheese, crumbled, or 75g (3oz)
freshly grated Parmesan cheese
50g (2oz) butter, softened
salt and freshly ground black pepper

Prepare the barbecue for grilling, following the instructions on **page 12**.

Season the noisettes with salt and pepper. Grill on one side, over medium heat, for about 8 minutes.

Blend the cheese and butter together with salt and pepper and set aside. Grill the other sides of the noisettes for about 5 minutes and then spread with the cheese mixture. Grill for a further 2–3 minutes. Serve immediately.

Mint jelly glazed breast of lamb

A cheap, but nonetheless very tasty cut, that barbecues well. Apart from the bones, remember to remove the tough membrane.

Serves 4

1 large, boned breast of lamb weighing
about 750g (1^1/$_2$ lb)
75g (3oz) fresh white breadcrumbs
^{1}/$_2$ teaspoon concentrated mint sauce
grated zest and juice of 1 lemon
1 egg, beaten
mint jelly, for glazing
salt and freshly ground black pepper
chopped fresh parsley, to garnish

Prepare the barbecue for 'Indirect heat' cooking, following the instructions on **page 14**.

Season the breast of lamb with salt and pepper.

Mix together the breadcrumbs, mint sauce, lemon zest and juice and enough of the beaten egg to make a fairly stiff mixture.

Spread the mixture evenly over the cut side of the meat. Roll up the breast tightly and secure with strong string every 2.5cm (1 inch) along the roll.

Place on the grill and cook over medium heat for about 1^1/$_4$ hours or until done to your liking. Spread a thin layer of mint jelly over the surface of the roll during the last 5–10 minutes of cooking time. Allow the meat to stand for about 10 minutes.

To serve, carve the meat into thick slices and scatter over the chopped parsley.

Spit-roasted chilli-stuffed leg of lamb

Serves 8

Rotisserie cooking is surely one of the most convivial barbecuing techniques. As the rotisserie is carrying out its task, the cook is free to relax with his or her guests. If your barbecue does not have a spit-roast assembly, you can roast the joint in a lidded barbecue, allowing approximately 22–25 minutes per 500g (1lb).

2.75kg (6 lb) leg of lamb, boned
50g (2oz) butter, melted

For the stuffing:
1 green pepper, finely chopped
3 medium onions, finely chopped
3 garlic cloves, finely chopped
2 small dried red chillies
2 teaspoons ground cumin
1/2 teaspoon salt
1 teaspoon freshly ground black pepper

Prepare the barbecue for spit-roasting, following the instructions on **page 17**.

Combine the stuffing ingredients and grind them into a paste (a pestle and mortar is ideal for this task but you can use a food processor if you prefer). Spread the paste evenly over the inside of the boned leg.

Roll up the meat as tightly as possible, from its narrowest point to its widest edge, and tie securely with fine string every 2.5cm (1 inch) along the length of the roll.

Position the stuffed joint on the spit, balance it (see page 18), and secure firmly with the spit forks.

Place the spit in position on the barbecue, turn on the motor, and again check that the joint turns evenly. Cook for about 1¹/₂–2 hours, occasionally basting the meat with the butter during the first 30 minutes or so of cooking. If you prefer your lamb slightly pink in the centre, it should be ready when a meat thermometer, pushed into the centre of the thickest part of the joint registers 60–65°C (140–150°F). A reading of 71°C (160°F) will indicate medium-done meat whilst 77°C (170°F) will indicate that it is well-done.

Leave the cooked joint to rest for 10–15 minutes before carving.

Sweet & sour shoulder of lamb

Serves 6

1.75–2.25kg (4–5 lb) shoulder of lamb
salt and freshly ground black pepper

For the sweet and sour glaze:
2 tablespoons red wine vinegar
1 tablespoon soy sauce
2 tablespoons apple or orange juice
1 tablespoon tomato purée
1 tablespoon mirin or dry sherry
1 garlic clove, very finely chopped
a pinch of ground ginger

Combine all the ingredients for the glaze and put to one side.

Prepare the barbecue for 'Indirect heat' cooking, following the instructions on **page 14**.

Season the shoulder with salt and pepper. Place the shoulder, fat side up, on the grill. Cook, with medium heat, for about 1^1/$_2$ hours. (The exact time will depend on the shoulder weight and the required degree of cooking.) Half an hour before the end of cooking, brush the shoulder generously with the prepared glaze.

Allow the lamb to rest for about 15 minutes before carving.

Butterflied leg of lamb in a herb crust

Apart from having to remove the bone (your butcher will do this for you if you ask him nicely) and having to stand duty whilst the meat is cooking, this is a great way to tackle a leg of lamb on your barbecue.

Serves 6–8

2.25–2.75kg (5–6 lb) leg of lamb
1 tablespoon chopped fresh rosemary
1 tablespoon chopped fresh parsley
1 tablespoon very finely chopped dried onion
1 tablespoon dried whole marjoram
1 large bay leaf, finely crumbled
^{1}/$_4$ teaspoon ground ginger
1 teaspoon salt
2 tablespoons red or white wine vinegar
50g (2oz) brown sugar
150ml (^{1}/$_4$ pint) dry white or red wine
150ml (^{1}/$_4$ pint) chicken stock

To butterfly the leg of lamb, cut down the length of the inside of the leg, carefully trim the flesh from the bone and remove the bone. Then open out the leg meat and, if necessary, slash the thicker areas to help the meat lie flat.

Combine all the remaining ingredients in a pan and heat gently for 20 minutes, stirring the sauce occasionally. Brush the sauce all over the meat.

Prepare the barbecue for grilling, following the instructions on **page 12**.

Place the meat on the grill, with the uncut surface (the fat side) uppermost. Cook over medium heat for about 40–50 minutes, or until cooked to your taste, basting it frequently with the sauce and turning the lamb occasionally. When cooked it should have a scrumptious, somewhat crusty-looking surface.
To serve, slice the lamb thinly across the grain.

Crown of roast lamb

A culinary work of art and a truly regal dish fit to grace any table. It is wise to order a crown from your butcher well in advance, but it is not all that difficult, albeit a little time-consuming, to make up your own from two matching racks of lamb, as described below.

Serves 6

2 racks of lamb
salt and freshly ground black pepper

For the stuffing:
25g (1oz) butter
1 small onion, finely chopped
1 large cooking apple, peeled, cored and finely chopped
250g (8oz) pork sausagemeat
3 tablespoons fresh white breadcrumbs, lightly toasted
1 tablespoon finely chopped fresh parsley
40g (1^1/$_2$ oz) walnuts, finely chopped
^{1}/$_2$ teaspoon dried thyme

With a sharp, short-bladed knife, trim the meat and fat 4cm (1^1/$_2$ inches) from the end of the rib bones on each joint and season with salt and pepper. Using a trussing needle and fine string, sew the ends of the joints together back to back so the fat is inside and the bones curve upwards and outwards.

To make the stuffing, melt the butter in a pan and cook the onion gently until soft. Add the apple and continue cooking for a few minutes. Add the sausagemeat and combine well with the onion and apple. Cook for a further 3–4 minutes. Stir in the breadcrumbs, parsley, walnuts and thyme.

Prepare the barbecue for 'Indirect heat' cooking, following the instructions on **page 14**.

Place the crown roast on a piece of foil slightly wider than the base of the roast. Spoon the stuffing into the cavity up to 2.5cm (1 inch) or so below the base of the trimmed bones (to allow space for the stuffing to rise). Cover the tips of the rib bones with foil to prevent charring.

Cook the lamb on the foil with medium heat, allowing 35 minutes per 500g (1 lb). For an unstuffed crown roast, allow 30 minutes per 500g (1 lb).

To serve, stand the crown on a serving dish and remove the foil from each bone tip. Allow 2 cutlets for each person.

Spit-roasted leg of lamb with anchovies, garlic & rosemary

Serves 8–10

2.25–2.75kg (5–6 lb) leg of lamb
4 garlic cloves, sliced lengthways into 3
2 x 50g (2oz) cans of anchovies in oil, drained
12 small sprigs of rosemary
75g (3oz) unsalted butter, softened
juice of 1 lemon
freshly ground black pepper

Using a narrow-bladed sharp knife, make 12 deep incisions into the fleshy side of the joint. Insert into each of these a garlic slice, half an anchovy and a sprig of rosemary, making sure they are well pushed in. Cream the remaining anchovies, butter and lemon juice together and spread the mixture over the joint. Grind pepper over the buttered joint.

Prepare the barbecue for spit-roasting, following the instructions on **page 17**.

Insert the spit almost parallel to the bone and test for balance (see page 18) before tightening the spit forks. Cook the joint over medium heat, basting the meat once or twice with some of the juices from the drip pan. If you prefer your meat done slightly pink in the centre, cook it for about 1¹⁄₄–1¹⁄₂ hours or until the temperature reading on a meat thermometer is 60–65°C (140–150°F). A reading of 71°C (160°F) will indicate medium-done meat whilst 77°C (170°F) will indicate that it is well-done.

Remove the joint from the spit, cover with foil and leave to rest for 15–20 minutes before carving.

Lambs kidney brochettes with sauce Bercy

To add a little 'je ne sais quoi' to this recipe, or indeed any other skewered lamb meat or offal dish, replace metal skewers with sharpened branches from a mature rosemary bush. Leaving some leaves at the unsharpened ends will not only help to provide a pleasant aroma during cooking, but will also prettify an otherwise plain offering.

Serves 4

12 lamb's kidneys
3 tablespoons melted butter

For the sauce Bercy:
75g (3oz) butter
1 tablespoon very finely chopped shallots
300ml (¹⁄₂ pint) dry white wine
2 teaspoons plain flour
1 tablespoon very finely chopped fresh parsley
salt and freshly ground black pepper

Remove the fat and fine skin from the kidneys. Split each one from the inside edge to within 1cm (¹⁄₂ inch) of the outer surface. Remove the white core from the inside. Thread the opened-out kidneys onto fine skewers using a wide 'stitch' across the back to hold them open.

Prepare the barbecue for grilling, following the instructions on **page 12**.

Prepare the sauce. Melt 25g (1oz) of the butter in a saucepan, add the shallots and cook until soft. Add the wine and simmer until the liquid has reduced by half. Mix the remaining butter and the flour to a paste and add a little at a time to the wine mixture. Cook, stirring, until the mixture thickens. Stir in the parsley and season to taste. Keep warm while cooking the kidneys.

Brush the kidneys with half the melted butter and grill over medium to high heat for about 3 minutes on each side, basting occasionally with the remaining butter. Do not overcook as kidneys can rapidly become tough. Serve with the sauce.

Herb-stuffed lamb's kidneys

Serves 4

12 lamb's kidneys
12 rashers of prime streaky bacon
40g (1¹/₂oz) butter, melted
fresh watercress, to garnish

For the herb stuffing:
75g (3oz) fresh white breadcrumbs
3 tablespoons chopped fresh mixed herbs
(including parsley)
25g (1oz) butter
1 medium onion, chopped
1 large egg, beaten
salt and freshly ground black pepper

Remove the fat and fine skin from the kidneys. Partially slit each one lengthways and remove the core. Remove the rind from the bacon rashers and spread them out on a work surface.

To make the stuffing, mix the breadcrumbs and herbs together. Melt the butter in a pan and cook the onion until soft. Stir the onion mixture into the breadcrumbs and add enough beaten egg to bind the mixture. Season well.

Prepare the barbecue for grilling, following the instructions on **page 12**.

Spoon the prepared stuffing into the kidneys, place each kidney at one end of a bacon rasher and roll up the rasher to enclose the kidney.

Thread the wrapped kidneys onto skewers and brush well with the melted butter. Grill over medium to high heat for about 4–5 minutes on each side, or until the bacon starts to crisp. Do not overcook otherwise the kidneys will become tough and chewy. Serve immediately, garnished with watercress.

Caul-wrapped marinated lamb's liver

Caul, a lace-like membrane of pork or lamb's fat, can be obtained from most butchers. For culinary purposes it is used to provide some protection, to offal in particular, from oven or grill heat whilst at the same time acting as a natural fat baster.

Serves 4–6

fresh or dry-salted caul, preferably pork
500–750g (1–1¹/₂ lb) lamb's liver, in one piece
red wine vinegar, to serve
freshly ground black pepper, to serve

For the marinade:
2 teaspoons paprika
¹/₂ teaspoon cumin
pinch of cayenne pepper
1 teaspoon salt
2 teaspoons lemon juice
3 tablespoons olive oil

If the caul is dry-salted, soak it in cold water for about 20 minutes to soften it. Remove it from the water and pat dry before use. Combine the marinade ingredients in a large bowl and mix well.

Peel away the outer membrane from the liver and cut away any coarse tubes or fibrous connective tissue. Add the liver to the marinade and leave for about 30 minutes in a cool place.

Prepare the barbecue for grilling, following the instructions on page 12.

Remove the liver from the marinade, reserving the marinade. Drain the liver and wrap it in the sheet of caul until it is completely enclosed. Cook the wrapped liver, over medium heat, for about 10 minutes on each side until nicely browned. Baste occasionally with the reserved marinade during cooking. The liver should be cooked when it feels firm when pressed lightly.

Leave the liver to rest in a warm place for about 10 minutes before carving into thick slices (the heart of the liver should be pink and juicy). Provide your guests with some red wine vinegar and freshly ground black pepper for sprinkling over the liver. Serve with a plain green salad.

beef & veal

Hot 'n' spicy bumper burger; Red wine burgers; Chuck-wagon Hamburgers; Rib eye steaks with rosemary; Stuffed rump steak with tarragon & parsley butter; Steak with blue cheese butter; Steak au poivre flambé; Teriyaki beef strips; Quick-fried beef with Chinese leaves; Stir-fried steak in oyster sauce; Teriyaki flank steak; Beef & courgette kebabs; Roast beef; Barbecued boeuf en croûte; Brandied sirloin, spit-roasted with a mustard coating; Stuffed veal chops; Roast veal; Veal & streaky kebabs; Skewered veal & ham olives.

Hot 'n' spicy bumper burger

A giant burger that will provide up to eight people with something to get their teeth into.

Serves 6–8

1 flat, round loaf of bread, about 25cm (10 inches) in diameter, or 2 pitta breads
1 quantity of Garlic butter or Tarragon & parsley butter (see pages 163 and 164), at room temperature
1kg (2 lb) chuck steak, finely minced
1 large onion, finely chopped
$1/2$ teaspoon mustard powder
1 tablespoon soy sauce
1 tablespoon chilli sauce
2 teaspoons horseradish sauce
$1/4$ teaspoon ground ginger
1 tablespoon Worcestershire sauce
1 large red onion, thinly sliced (optional)
2 large tomatoes, thinly sliced
1 avocado, thinly sliced
shredded lettuce

Slice the loaf in half horizontally. If using pitta breads, part-slice these horizontally and lift open to make a large, hinged flat bread. Spread the cut surfaces of the bread with the flavoured butter.

In a large bowl mix together the meat, onion, mustard, soy sauce, chilli sauce, horseradish sauce, ginger and Worcestershire sauce. Shape the mixture into a large burger slightly bigger in diameter than the loaf or opened-out pitta bread.

Prepare the barbecue for grilling, following the instructions on **page 12**.

Place the burger directly on the grill or griddle plate. Cook the burger over high heat for 6–10 minutes on each side or until cooked to the desired degree. Use 2 rimless baking sheets – one slipped under the burger and one on top – to turn the burger.

Once the burger has been turned, place the bread, cut sides down, to toast on the grill.

To serve, place the burger on one of the toasted sides of the loaf or pitta breads and top with the onion slices (if using), tomatoes, avocado, shredded lettuce and remaining bread, toasted side down. Cut into the required number of wedges and serve immediately.

Red wine burgers

Serves 6–8

5 tablespoons red wine
50g (2oz) butter
2 medium onions, finely chopped
750g (1¹/₂ lb) chuck steak, finely minced
40g (1¹/₂oz) fresh white breadcrumbs
1 teaspoon salt
¹/₄ teaspoon freshly ground black pepper
1 egg, beaten
6–8 soft rolls, halved, to serve

Prepare the barbecue for grilling, following the instructions on **page 12**.

Lightly mix half of the wine, butter and onions into the meat, setting aside the remaining wine, butter and onions. Stir in the breadcrumbs, salt, pepper and egg. Shape the mixture into 6–8 burgers approximately 2cm (³/₄ inch) thick.

Melt the reserved butter in a small saucepan, add the reserved onion and fry gently until transparent. Add the reserved wine and simmer for about 5 minutes. Brush the wine sauce over the burgers and grill, or cook on the griddle plate, over medium to high heat, for about 8–10 minutes on each side. Brush the sauce over the burgers occasionally during cooking. Toast the cut sides of the rolls during the last few minutes of cooking. Place the burgers in the rolls and serve.

Chuck-wagon hamburgers

Serves 6

A classic 'stretched burger' recipe that smells as yummy as it tastes! For an added flavour boost, melt a slice of mature Cheddar on top during the final few minutes of grilling.

1 small onion, finely chopped
1 green pepper, finely chopped
2 medium carrots, grated
1 garlic clove, crushed
500g (1lb) chuck steak, finely minced
2 teaspoons Worcestershire sauce
3 tablespoons vegetable oil
50g (2oz) fresh white breadcrumbs
1 teaspoon salt
1 teaspoon freshly ground pepper
1 egg, lightly beaten
6 soft rolls, halved, to serve
2 large tomatoes, sliced, to serve

Prepare the barbecue for grilling, following the instructions on **page 12**.

Sauté the onion, green pepper, carrots and garlic in a pan until softened and drain well on kitchen paper.

In a large bowl, lightly but thoroughly mix together the sautéed vegetables with the steak, Worcestershire sauce, oil, breadcrumbs, and salt and pepper. Bind together the mixture with the beaten egg before shaping into 6 burgers approximately 2cm (³/₄inch) thick. If necessary, drain the burgers on kitchen paper.

Cook on the grill or griddle plate, over medium to high heat, for about 8–10 minutes on each side. Ensure the burgers are cooked through and the centres are piping hot.

During the final few minutes of cooking, toast the cut sides of the rolls on the barbecue grill. Top each burger with a tomato slice and serve immediately in a toasted roll.

Rib eye steaks with rosemary

Serves 4

4 rib eye steaks cut 2–2.5cm ($^3/_4$–1 inch) thick
1 tablespoon olive oil
2 tablespoons chopped fresh rosemary
salt and freshly ground pepper

Brush the steaks all over with the oil and press equal quantities of the rosemary into both sides. Leave the steaks at room temperature for about 30 minutes.

Prepare the barbecue for grilling, following the instructions on **page 12**.

Grill the steaks over medium heat until cooked to the desired degree. Carefully turn them over, halfway through cooking. Season with salt and pepper and serve with salad or vegetables in season.

To provide each of your guests with a steak cooked to suit their individual requirements, try cutting the steaks to different thicknesses before proceeding to cook them in concert, i.e. if the steaks are placed on the grill together and come off the grill at the same time, and you use the chart on page 182 as a guide, you should – all being well – end up by serving rare, medium or well-done steaks to order. The 'well-doners' might, however, object to the 'under-doners' getting a bigger slice of the cake!

Stuffed rump steak with tarragon & parsley butter

Serves 4

750g (1$^1/_2$ lb) rump steak,
cut about 4cm (1$^1/_2$ inches) thick
1 quantity of Tarragon & parsley butter
(see page 164), chilled
oil for brushing

For the stuffing:
1 teaspoon finely chopped shallot or onion
1 tablespoon olive oil
125g (4oz) open mushrooms, finely chopped
1 teaspoon finely chopped fresh parsley
1 garlic clove, crushed
1 rounded tablespoon finely chopped cooked ham
1 tablespoon fresh white breadcrumbs
salt and freshly ground black pepper

To prepare the stuffing, in a pan cook the shallot or onion in the oil until soft. Add the mushrooms, parsley and garlic, cover the pan and cook over medium heat for about 5 minutes. Add the ham, breadcrumbs and salt and pepper and stir lightly to mix. Tip the mixture onto a plate to cool.

Prepare the barbecue for grilling, following the instructions on **page 12**.

Slit the steak along the side to form a deep pocket. Push the stuffing well into the pocket and close the opening with a trussing needle and string or a fine skewer. Slice the butter into pats. Brush the steak with oil and grill over medium to high heat for about 4–5 minutes on each side, or until cooked to the desired degree. Remove the string or skewer. Cut the steak into 1cm ($^1/_2$ inch) slices and serve with the flavoured butter.

Steak with blue cheese butter

Serves 4–6

750g (1^1/$_2$ lb) whole flank steak
175ml (6floz) good-quality shop-bought
French dressing
1 tablespoon soft butter
75g (3oz) blue cheese
1 tablespoon finely chopped chives
1 garlic clove, very finely chopped
1 tablespoon chopped fresh rosemary
or 1 teaspoon dried rosemary
a pinch of dried oregano or dried basil
a pinch of freshly ground black pepper

Place the steak in a shallow dish and pour over the French dressing. Turn the steak 2 or 3 times; then cover and place in the refrigerator for at least 4 hours or overnight.

Blend together the butter, blue cheese, chives, garlic, rosemary, oregano or basil and pepper. Chill if not using immediately.

Prepare the barbecue for grilling, following the instructions on **page 12**.

Lift the steak from the dish and drain briefly. Grill over high heat for 4–5 minutes per side – depending on the thickness of the steak. For best eating, the steak should be served rare (medium and well-done flank usually ends up being somewhat tough). Place the steak on a warm platter and slice thinly across the grain at an angle of 45 degrees.

Serve with a pat or spoonful of the blue cheese butter melting over each portion. This is delicious served with a simple **Tomato and onion salad** (see page 129).

Steak au poivre flambé

This recipe provides the cook with a great opportunity to add a little extra drama and excitement to his, or her, barbecue performance.

Serves 4

2 tablespoons black peppercorns, coarsely crushed
4 fillet or rump steaks about 2.5cm (1 inch) thick
50g (2oz) butter
2 large tomatoes, thickly sliced
a pinch of fresh or dried oregano
a pinch of garlic salt
4 tablespoons brandy

Press the peppercorns firmly into both sides of the steaks. Leave the steaks at room temperature for 30–40 minutes.

Prepare the barbecue for grilling, following the instructions on **page 12**.

Grill the steaks over high heat until cooked to the desired degree (about 5 minutes per side for rare). When cooked, transfer the meat to a hot, shallow dish.

Melt the butter in a frying pan, add the tomato slices and heat through. Season with the oregano and garlic salt. Arrange the tomato slices on top of the steaks. Warm the brandy, spoon it evenly over the steaks and ignite. Serve as soon as the flames subside.

Teriyaki beef strips

Serves 6–8

1kg (2 lb) sirloin steak 2cm ($3/4$ inch) thick, cut into 6mm ($1/4$ inch) thick slices
oil for greasing skewers

For the marinade:
6 tablespoons soy sauce or shoyu sauce
2 tablespoons red wine, red wine vinegar or sake
1 teaspoon ground ginger
$1^1/2$ tablespoons groundnut oil
1 garlic clove, very finely chopped
1–3 teaspoons soft brown sugar, to taste

To make the marinade, mix together the ingredients in a bowl. Add the meat slices and turn until well coated with the marinade. Cover the bowl and place in the refrigerator for 3–4 hours.

Prepare the barbecue for grilling, following the instructions on **page 12**.

Lift the meat out of the bowl, drain briefly and reserve the marinade. Thread the meat, snake-like, onto 15–20cm (6–8 inch) long, oiled metal skewers. Grill the meat over medium to high heat for just 1–2 minutes on each side, basting once or twice with the marinade. Serve immediately.

Quick-fried beef with Chinese leaves

Quick, easy and tasty. All in all, quite a 'stirring' little recipe!

Serves 4

500g (1 lb) fillet or rump steak
750g (1½ lb) Chinese lettuce leaves
4 tablespoons vegetable oil
3 teaspoons cornflour
3 tablespoons oyster sauce
1 teaspoon sesame oil
½ teaspoon sugar
2 tablespoons cold water
salt and freshly ground black pepper

For the marinade:
1 teaspoon sake or dry sherry
1 teaspoon soy sauce
½ teaspoon sugar
1 teaspoon sesame oil
1 medium egg yolk

Prepare the barbecue for wok-cooking, following the instructions on **page 19**.

Combine all the marinade ingredients in a bowl.

Slice the beef into thin slices (part-freezing the meat beforehand will help) about 5–6cm (2–2½ inches) in length. Add to the bowl and leave to marinate in a cool place for about an hour.

Cut the Chinese leaves into 5cm (2 inch) lengths.

Position the wok on the barbecue and heat 2 tablespoons of the vegetable oil in it. Add the Chinese leaves and stir-fry over a high heat until tender. Season the leaves and arrange over the bottom of a large platter. Drain the beef from the marinade, sprinkle over the cornflour and mix together. Heat the remaining vegetable oil in the wok and stir-fry the beef strips until golden brown. Remove the beef from the wok and keep warm. Add the oyster sauce to the wok, and when it begins to bubble, return the beef to the wok along with the sesame oil, sugar and 2 tablespoons water. Keep stirring until the sauce thickens and the beef is heated through.

Scatter the beef over the Chinese leaves and serve immediately.

Stir-fried steak in oyster sauce

Serves 4–6

750g ($1^1/_2$ lb) fillet or rump steak, thinly sliced
1 tablespoon cornflour
$^1/_2$ teaspoon salt
4 tablespoons groundnut oil
1 tablespoon soy sauce
2 tablespoons oyster sauce
$^1/_2$ chicken stock cube, crushed
2 tablespoons dry sherry
freshly ground black pepper
2 spring onions, finely sliced, to garnish
1 red chilli, finely sliced, to garnish (optional)

Prepare the barbecue for wok-cooking, following the instructions on **page 19**.

Cut the steaks across the grain into 5cm (2 inch) strips the thickness of a pencil. Sprinkle with the cornflour and salt, add a little pepper, and mix together lightly.

Heat the wok on the barbecue, add the oil, and when very hot add the beef, spreading the strips evenly. Stir-fry over high heat for 1 minute. Add the soy and oyster sauces, stock cube and sherry. Stir-fry for a further minute and then turn out onto a warmed dish, with the spring onions and chilli, if using, scattered over. Serve immediately with plain rice or noodles.

Teriyaki flank steak

This recipe is best with thick flank, so request this from your butcher. Teriyaki flank steak sandwiches are hard to beat, be the meat hot or cold.

Serves 4–6

750g (1¹/₂ lb) whole flank steak

For the marinade:
6 tablespoons soy sauce
150ml (¹/₄ pint) red wine or red wine vinegar
2 teaspoons freshly grated root ginger
1 garlic clove, very finely chopped
2 tablespoons light muscovado sugar
2 tablespoons lemon juice
2 tablespoons groundnut oil
1 medium onion, finely chopped
¹/₄ teaspoon freshly ground black pepper

Give the steak a firm beating with a rolling pin or wooden steak hammer. Place the steak in a shallow dish. Mix together all the ingredients for the marinade and pour over the meat. Cover and leave in the refrigerator for at least 6 hours or overnight.

Prepare the barbecue for grilling, following the instructions on **page 12**.

Lift the steak from the marinade and drain briefly. Reserve the marinade. Place the steak on the grill or griddle plate and cook over high heat for about 5 minutes on each side, basting occasionally with the marinade. (Flank should only be served rare as medium-to-well-done steaks can turn out a little leathery.) To serve the steak, slice it thinly at an angle of 45 degrees.

Beef & courgette kebabs

Serves 4

2 courgettes
3 tablespoons groundnut oil, plus extra for greasing skewers
3 tablespoons soft butter
1 garlic clove, crushed
¹/₄ teaspoon freshly ground black pepper
1kg (2 lb) rump, sirloin or fillet steak, trimmed and cut into 2.5cm (1 inch) cubes
4 medium tomatoes, quartered

Slice the courgettes into circles about 1cm (1 inch) thick. Blanch them in a pan of boiling water for 30 seconds. Drain well.

Prepare the barbecue for grilling, following the instructions on **page 12**.

Place the oil, butter, garlic and pepper in a small saucepan and heat gently for a few minutes. Keep the pan on the side of the grill for basting.

Thread the meat cubes, courgette slices and tomato quarters alternately onto oiled metal skewers and brush with the garlic oil. Grill over medium to high heat, turning and basting frequently, for about 10 minutes or until cooked to the desired degree.

Roast beef

Opening up the lid of your barbecue to reveal a delectable fore rib in all its glory, is guaranteed to create havoc with bystanders' taste buds! The visual impact will be compounded if a golden mound of Yorkshire pudding can be glimpsed beneath the grill bars.

Fore rib or wing rib (with bone in,
allow about 375g/12oz per serving,
if joint is boned and rolled,
allow about 250g/8oz per serving)

Trim any excess fat from the meat, wipe the joint and rub salt and pepper into it. Securely tie the joint with twine at 2.5cm (1 inch) intervals.

Prepare the barbecue for 'Indirect heat' cooking, following the instructions on **page 14**.

Roast the meat, with a medium heat, until cooked to the desired degree. See the roasting time chart on page 181 for further information.

Should you wish to offer Yorkshire pudding to your family and guests, make up your usual pudding mix about an hour or so before the roast has finished cooking. Having allowed the pudding mixture to stand for about 30 minutes or so, gently pour it through the grill bars of the barbecue into the drip pan containing the hot fats and juices that have fallen from the joint above.

Continue cooking, with the lid of the barbecue in the closed position, for the last 30 minutes of cooking time or until the pudding has become puffed up and golden.

Allow the joint to rest for at least 10 minutes to allow the juices to settle before carving.

Barbecued boeuf en croûte

Boeuf en croûte (beef Wellington) is a spectacular dish to serve up at dinner parties and relatively easy to prepare. Although somewhat expensive when compared to other dishes, the cost per head compares very favourably to providing each guest with, say, a decent-sized pizza. Apart from beef, barbecuing 'en croûte' can be applied to boned venison, lamb, chicken or large fish such as salmon and sea trout.

I recommend that the preparation is carried out the day before the event, but it can be carried out on the actual day, providing the part-cooked meat is quite cold and the pastry well chilled before preparing the dish.

Serves 6

1kg (2 lb) fillet of beef
brandy for brushing
75g (3oz) butter
1 Spanish onion, finely chopped
250g (8oz) closed-cap button mushrooms, finely chopped
2 teaspoons chopped mixed fresh herbs
500g (1 lb) packet of puff pastry, well chilled
1 egg, well beaten
a little red wine
salt and freshly ground black pepper
fresh watercress or parsley, to garnish

The day before, or early on the day itself, pre-heat the oven to Gas Mark 7/220°C/425°F.

Trim the excess fat from the fillet and tie the meat into a compact shape. Brush the fillet generously with brandy.

Melt 25g (1oz) of the butter over a medium heat in a roasting tin. Increase the heat, add the meat and brown it quickly all over. Then roast the meat in the oven for 15 minutes, basting it occasionally with the pan juices.

Remove the meat from the oven and allow it to get cold. Remove the string and place the meat in the refrigerator. Reserve the pan juices for making gravy.

The next day, melt the remaining butter in a small saucepan, add the onion and cook for about 5 minutes. Add the mushrooms and mixed herbs and continue cooking over a gentle heat until the mixture is fairly concentrated (this takes about 20 minutes). Season the mixture with salt and pepper and set aside to cool.

Prepare the barbecue for 'Indirect heat' cooking, following the instructions on **page 14.**

Roll out the pastry to a rectangle, about 38 x 25cm (15 x 10 inches), reserving the edge trimmings for decoration. Spread half the mushroom mixture over the centre of the pastry and place the meat on top. Spread the remaining mushroom mixture over the fillet. Brush the edge of the pastry with some of the beaten egg and wrap the pastry around the fillet, pressing the edges firmly together. Brush any excess pastry at the ends with more of the egg and double-fold. Cut out diamond shapes from the reserved pastry, moisten with more of the beaten egg and use to decorate the pastry. Brush the pastry all over with the rest of the egg.

Carefully place the pastry-wrapped beef on a baking sheet and bake, with medium to high heat, for 35–40 minutes, or until the pastry is well browned.

Add some red wine to the reserved pan juices and simmer to reduce slightly. Keep warm.

Cut the beef into thick slices and serve it, garnished with watercress or parsley, with the gravy.

Brandied sirloin, spit-roasted with a mustard coating

Serves 6–8

1.25–1.75kg (3–4 lb) sirloin of beef

For the marinade:
4 tablespoons brandy
150ml (1/4 pint) apple juice
150ml (1/4 pint) sunflower oil
2 garlic cloves, very finely chopped
1/4 teaspoon freshly ground black pepper

For the mustard coating:
2 tablespoons wholegrain mustard
1/2 teaspoon freshly ground black pepper
55ml (2fl oz) single cream

Combine the marinade ingredients and stir well. Place the meat in a baking dish and pour the marinade over. Cover with cling film and leave the meat, turning it occasionally, to marinate in the refrigerator overnight, or for as long as possible on the day of cooking.

Prepare the barbecue for spit-roasting, following the instructions on **page 17**.

Remove the meat from the marinade, drain briefly and pat dry with kitchen paper. Insert the spit through the centre of the sirloin and test for balance (see page 18) before tightening the spit forks. If deemed necessary, tie the meat securely with string at regular intervals to retain the shape of the joint.

Prepare the mustard coating by combining the mustard, pepper and cream. Spread the paste evenly over the surface of the meat. Position a drip pan to catch the juices falling from the meat as it rotates.

Cook the sirloin over medium heat. Cooking time will depend upon all the usual variables, i.e. weight of the joint, desired degree of doneness, lid set in the open or closed position and the state of the weather, but for rare to medium meat reckon on 2–2 1/2 hours. Otherwise test with a meat thermometer until the reading registers around 65°C (150°F).

If desired, skim the fats from the roasting juices and whisk together with some of the reserved marinade to serve separately as a sauce.

Stuffed veal chops

Serves 4

4 x 2.5cm (1 inch) thick veal chops
4 very thin bacon rashers
4 slices of Gruyère or Fontina cheese
1 tablespoon chopped fresh thyme or rosemary
oil for brushing
a pinch of grated nutmeg
salt and freshly ground black pepper

Prepare the barbecue for grilling, following the instructions on **page 12**.

Cut a deep pocket, almost to the bone, through the thick part of each chop. Slide a rasher of bacon and a slice of cheese into each pocket, together with a sprinkling of the chopped herbs.

Lay the chops on a board and beat the open edges hard with a rolling pin or meat hammer. Brush the chops with oil and season with salt, pepper and grated nutmeg.

Grill the chops over medium heat for about 8 minutes on each side or until the cheese begins to melt and run out of the chops. Serve immediately.

Roast veal

Serve this with veal forcemeat or stuffing balls, and cook them alongside the roast during the last 40 minutes or so of cooking.

Serves 6

1.75kg (4 lb) loin, leg or shoulder of veal, boned and rolled
flour for sprinkling
8 rashers of streaky bacon
50g (2oz) fat, preferably dripping
salt and freshly ground black pepper

Stand the veal in a roasting tin, sprinkle with flour and season lightly with salt and pepper. Lay the rashers of bacon evenly over the veal and spread the fat liberally over the whole joint.

Prepare the barbecue for 'Indirect heat' cooking, following the instructions on **page 14**.

Roast the veal, with medium to high heat, for about 20 minutes; then lower the heat to medium if using a gas barbecue, or remove some of the charcoal fire-bed, for the remaining cooking period. A 1.75kg (4 lb) veal joint should take $1^3/_4$–2 hours to cook until well done. Allow the joint to rest for about 10 minutes before carving.

Veal & streaky kebabs

Serves 4

500g (1 lb) lean shoulder of veal or veal fillet
6 rashers of streaky bacon
250g (8oz) button mushrooms
1 large green pepper, de-seeded, grilled and skinned, cut into 2.5cm (1 inch) squares
a pinch of ground ginger
a pinch of ground mace
a pinch of ground nutmeg
75g (3oz) butter
oil for greasing skewers
salt and freshly ground black pepper

Prepare the barbecue for grilling, following the instructions on **page 12**.

Cut the veal into 2–2.5cm ($^3/_4$–1 inch) cubes. Roll up each rasher of bacon and cut in half to make 2 rolls.

Thread the bacon, veal, mushrooms and green pepper onto oiled metal skewers, making sure that a roll of bacon is nestling against each cube of veal. Sprinkle the meat with the spices and salt and pepper and dot with the butter.

Grill over medium heat for about 15–20 minutes, turning the kebabs frequently, or until the bacon and veal are cooked.

Skewered veal & ham olives

This dish can also be made using escalopes of pork. I personally like the strong scent and flavour from the sage but, if preferred, use leaves of basil or mint.

Serves 4

4 thin veal escalopes, trimmed into 10–13cm (4–5 inch) squares
lemon juice, to taste
4 thin slices of cooked ham, trimmed into 10–13cm (4–5 inch) squares
4 thin rashers of streaky bacon
2 medium onions, cut into 5mm ($^1/_4$ inch) thick slices
handful of fresh sage leaves
2 tablespoons melted bacon fat or dripping
oil for greasing skewers
salt and freshly ground black pepper

Prepare the barbecue for grilling, following the instructions on **page 12**.

Season the escalopes with lemon juice and salt and pepper. Lay a slice of ham on each escalope. Roll up the meat and tightly wrap a piece of bacon around each roll.

Thread two veal and ham olives onto an oiled metal skewer or, preferably, use 2 skewers spaced about 4cm ($1^1/_2$ inches) apart, inserting one skewer through the right of each olive, and one through the left of each – so that the olives form the central 'crossbar' of the H (this just holds the olives more securely). Alternate each olive with a slice of onion and a sage leaf. Do the same with the other 2 olives.

Brush the olives with the bacon fat or dripping and grill over medium heat for about 8 minutes or until cooked through. Turn and baste a few times during cooking.

vegetables & salads

Parmesan parsnip puff; Leek, cheese & potato layer; Crêpes Julie; Ratatouille; Cheese & herb-stuffed tomatoes; Barbecued baked beans; Potato kebabs madras; Roasted potatoes with garlic, rosemary & thyme; Gratin dauphinoise; Herb & sesame new potatoes; Baked potatoes with toppings; Orange & ginger glazed carrots; Tomatoes provençale; Sweetcorn with dill; Bacon-wrapped corn; Roasted red peppers; Spicy nut roast; Mixed vegetable kebabs; Gem squash McTaggart; Helen Louise's fancy fried rice; Pilau rice; Saffron rice; Tomato & onion salad; Aubergine & pepper salad; Salade niçoise; Caesar salad; Brown rice & vegetable salad; Bean sprout salad with koi-kuchi-shoyu dressing; Oriental cucumber & radish salad; Potato salad; Mayonnaise.

Parmesan parsnip puff

Serves 4

I am particularly fond of the humble parsnip, a much underrated, umbelliferous vegetable that is seldom used by barbecue cooks. Roast parsnips, when baked in concert with roast potatoes (they take a little less cooking time), develop a delectable sweet crunchiness that I find exceedingly yummy. The recipe that follows, adapted for barbecue 'Indirect heat' cooking, looks lovely, tastes divine and goes down well with old and young alike.

900 g (2 lb) parsnips, peeled and cut into small cubes – young parsnips are best
50g (2oz) butter
4 tablespoons single cream
2 eggs, beaten
2 tablespoons freshly grated Parmesan cheese
a pinch of freshly grated nutmeg
salt and freshly ground black pepper

In a pan bring about 1 litre (1³/₄ pints) of water to boiling point. Add the parsnips and simmer, covered, for about 10 minutes or until tender when tested with a skewer.

Drain off all the water and allow to rest, with the lid on, for 10 minutes or so.

Thoroughly purée the parsnips, using a sieve or liquidiser. Beat half the butter into the purée and then add the cream, remaining eggs and nutmeg, and season with salt and pepper.

Use a little of the remaining butter to grease a shallow flameproof dish. Tip the mixture into the dish and dot with the rest of the butter. Sprinkle over the Parmesan.

Prepare the barbecue for 'Indirect heat' cooking, following the instructions on **page 14**.

Bake the 'puff' with medium to high heat for 25–30 minutes. The heat indicator on the lid of the barbecue (if it has one) should register around 220°C (425°F).

Serve immediately.

Leek, cheese & potato layer

Serves 4

500 g (1 lb) potatoes, preferably
King Edwards or Desiree or similar
2 tablespoons vegetable oil
2 medium leeks, sliced
1 large garlic clove, halved
butter for greasing
175 g (6 oz) Cheddar cheese, coarsely grated
3 medium eggs
250ml (8fl oz) milk
1 teaspoon dried mixed herbs
salt and freshly ground black pepper

Prepare the barbecue for 'Indirect heat' cooking, following the instructions on **page 14**.

Peel the potatoes and slice them very thinly (a mandoline is the ideal tool for this job). Briefly parboil the slices, drain and put to one side.

Heat the oil in a pan and gently fry the leeks until softened.

Rub the inside of a flameproof earthenware gratin dish, about 25 x 25cm (10 x 10 inches), with the cut garlic halves and grease the bottom and sides of the dish with butter. Place a layer of the potato slices in the dish, followed by a layer of the softened leeks then a light sprinkling of the grated Cheddar. Repeat the layering, finishing with the cheese.

Beat the eggs, milk, herbs and salt and pepper together and pour evenly over the layered vegetables.

Position the dish on the barbecue and cook with medium heat for about 40 minutes until the egg mixture has set and the top is golden.

Crêpes Julie

Serves 4

50g (2oz) plain flour
1/4 teaspoon salt
1 large egg, lightly beaten
3 tablespoons milk
2 tablespoons single cream
15g (1/2oz) butter, melted
225g (8oz) floury potatoes
olive oil for greasing
25g (1oz) butter
freshly ground black pepper

Sift the flour and salt into a bowl. Make a well in the centre and pour in the beaten egg. Using a wooden spoon, beat the mixture, gradually incorporating the milk and cream to make a smooth batter. Finally beat in the melted butter. Cover and leave for 30–40 minutes.

Meanwhile, thinly peel the potatoes and, using the large holes on a grater, grate the potatoes onto 3 layers of kitchen paper. Firmly pat the grated potato with a clean tea towel to remove as much of the juice as possible. Add the potatoes to the prepared batter, stir and season generously with freshly ground pepper.

Prepare the barbecue for grilling, following the instructions on **page 12**.

Lightly grease the barbecue's griddle plate or a large heavy-based frying pan with oil, and add half the butter.

Once the butter has melted, spoon 4 crêpes into the pan, using 2 tablespoons of potato batter mixture for each crêpe. Keep as much space between them as possible. Spread the batter in thin circles. If you are using a griddle plate, and there is sufficient room to accommodate 8 crêpes, add all the butter prior to cooking. Cook the crêpes over medium heat for about 5 minutes, or until the undersides are golden. Turn with a spatula and cook for a further 5 minutes or until crisp, golden and cooked through. Serve immediately.

Ratatouille

I am still unsure whether I prefer ratatouille hot or cold, but one thing is for sure, it certainly goes down well at any temperature with chicken, lamb, beef or fish – or just by itself.

Serves 4–6

1 medium aubergine
2 large onions
4 small courgettes
1 medium red pepper, de-seeded
1 medium green pepper, de-seeded
2 large tomatoes
6 tablespoons olive oil
3 garlic cloves, crushed
1 tablespoon chopped fresh basil
1 teaspoon dried rosemary
1 bay leaf
1 teaspoon salt
$1/2$ teaspoon freshly ground black pepper
2 tablespoons chopped fresh parsley

Prepare the barbecue for grilling, following the instructions on **page 12**.

Thinly slice the aubergine, onions and courgettes. Chop the red and green peppers. Remove the skins and seeds from the tomatoes and cut the flesh into wedges.

Place a large skillet or roasting tin on the grill and heat the oil over high heat. Add the onions and garlic and cook for about 5 minutes or until the onions are soft and translucent. Next add the aubergine, peppers and courgettes. Cook for another 5 minutes, shaking the skillet or stirring the contents of the roasting tin frequently.

Add the tomatoes, basil, rosemary, bay leaf, salt and pepper. Sprinkle over the parsley. Bring the lid of the barbecue down, reduce the heat to medium (if using a gas barbecue) and continue cooking for a further 50–60 minutes. Serve the ratatouille hot or cold, as a main dish or with chicken, lamb, fish or beef.

Cheese & herb-stuffed tomatoes

Serves 4

2 large firm tomatoes
3 tablespoons fresh white breadcrumbs
2 tablespoons finely chopped fresh parsley
1 small garlic clove, crushed
25g (1oz) grated cheese e.g. Cheddar, mozzarella
2 tablespoons softened butter
a pinch of dried basil

Prepare the barbecue for grilling, following the instructions on **page 12**.

Cut the tomatoes in half lengthways and scrape out the seeds using a teaspoon.

Combine the remaining ingredients and lightly pack the mixture into the tomato cavities. Place the tomato halves, cut sides up, on the grill and cook, over medium heat, for about 10 minutes or until the tomatoes are heated through and the cheese has melted.

Barbecued baked beans

Serves 4

125g (4oz) streaky bacon rashers, rinds removed
25g (1oz) butter
1 tablespoon olive oil
1 large onion, finely chopped
1 celery stick, finely chopped
475g (15oz) can of baked beans in tomato sauce
4 small frankfurter sausages
1 tablespoon horseradish sauce
2 tablespoons Worcestershire sauce
1 teaspoon Dijon mustard
3 tablespoons tomato ketchup
50g (2oz) soft dark brown sugar

Prepare the barbecue for grilling, following the instructions on **page 12**.

Cut the rashers of bacon into pieces about 2.5cm (1 inch) long. Put the bacon into a heavy-based saucepan and heat gently on the barbecue until the fat starts to run. Add the butter, oil, onion and celery and continue to cook gently until the onion is translucent and golden brown.

Put the remaining ingredients into the pan and heat through, stirring frequently. If you wish to give the beans a nice smoky flavour, drop a handful of soaked wood chips such as hickory, or perhaps some fresh herbs, onto the hot fire bed a few minutes before placing the pan. With the lid down (in between stirring), the aromatic smoke will help to give the beans a nice smoky flavour. Don't worry if the surface becomes a little dry and crusty – this will give an extra tang to the beans and help evoke images of chuck wagons of old trundling along the Chisholm Trail.

Potato kebabs madras

One of my favourite potato dishes. When cooked, the kebabs should have great eye appeal. Try ringing the changes with the curry to see which flavour/colour you prefer.

Serves 4

750g (1¹/₂ lb) new potatoes or main-crop potatoes, washed and cut into 2.5–4cm (1–1¹/₂ inch) cubes (leaving the skin on the potatoes will add to their flavour)
6 tablespoons bottled curry paste or curry powder blended with 2–3 tablespoons water
oil for greasing skewers
salt

Cook the potato cubes in boiling, salted water until they are barely tender but not overcooked – a fine skewer should push into a cube without undue pressure. Drain thoroughly. When the potatoes are cool enough to handle, thread the cubes onto oiled metal (preferably flat-bladed) skewers, leaving a small gap between each cube. Generously brush the cubes with the curry paste or blended curry powder and allow to stand for up to an hour.

Prepare the barbecue for grilling, following the instructions on **page 12**.

Grill over high heat for about 10 minutes or until the potato cubes are uniformly cooked on all sides. Baste the potatoes once or twice during cooking with any leftover paste. Serve immediately.

Roasted potatoes with garlic, rosemary & thyme

A cracking combination of taste, appearance and aroma. This dish also makes a great appetiser that is far more satisfying than a packet of crisps, even if the crisps are barbecue flavoured. (Pictured on page 55.)

You will need a shallow steel roasting-tin measuring approximately 30 x 40cm (12 x 16 inches).

Serves 4–6

1kg (2 lb) large new potatoes, washed, skins left on, cut into 1cm (¹/₂ inch) cubes
2 tablespoons fresh rosemary leaves, finely chopped
1 tablespoon fresh thyme leaves, stripped off the stems
2 garlic cloves, finely chopped
2 tablespoons olive oil
salt and freshly ground black pepper

Prepare the barbecue for 'Indirect heat' cooking, following the instructions on **page 14**.

Pour the oil into the roasting tin and place in the barbecue to heat up.

Thoroughly dry the potato cubes in a clean tea towel and transfer onto a tray or large plate. Having carefully pushed the roasting tin over the barbecue's fire-bed, equally carefully slide the potatoes into the hot oil. Replace the tin in its original position.

Stir the potatoes around whilst sprinkling over the rosemary, thyme and garlic. Continue cooking over high heat for 30–40 minutes or until the potatoes are golden brown. Season with salt and pepper and serve immediately.

Gratin dauphinoise

The vegetable equivalent of creamy rice pudding?

Serves 4–6

1kg (2 lb) potatoes, preferably Desiree or
King Edwards, or similar
1 large garlic clove, halved, plus 1 small garlic clove,
very finely chopped
25g (1oz) butter
freshly grated nutmeg, to taste
1 egg
250ml (8fl oz) hot milk
250ml (8fl oz) double cream
50g (2oz) Gruyère cheese, grated
salt and freshly ground black pepper

Prepare the barbecue for 'Indirect heat' cooking,
following the instructions on **page 14**.

Peel the potatoes and slice them very thinly (a
mandoline is perfect for this task). Plunge the potato
slices into a bowl of cold water and stir around to
wash off some of the starch. Drain and dry the slices
very thoroughly in a clean tea towel.

Rub the inside of a flameproof gratin dish with the
garlic halves and grease it with the butter. Place the
potato slices in layers, sprinkling each layer with the
finely chopped garlic and nutmeg, salt and pepper to
taste.

Whisk the egg, milk and cream together, and pour the
mixture over the potato slices, ensuring the top layer is
completely covered. Cover the top with the Gruyère.

Cook, with medium heat, for 1–1¼ hours or until the
potatoes are tender when pierced with a skewer.

Herb & sesame new potatoes

Serves 4–6

1kg (2 lb) new potatoes
50g (2oz) butter
1 tablespoon chopped fresh parsley
1 tablespoon chopped fresh mint
1 tablespoon sesame seeds, toasted
salt and freshly ground black pepper

Peel a 2.5cm (1 inch) strip from the circumference of
each potato.

Prepare the barbecue for grilling or 'Indirect heat'
cooking, following the instructions on **page 12** or **14**.

Grease a large piece of heavy-duty foil (or 2 layers of
ordinary foil) with about half the butter. Place the
potatoes together in the centre of the foil and season
with salt and pepper. Sprinkle over some of the herbs.
Wrap the foil securely around the potatoes, following
one of the methods outlined on page 20.

Cook for 40–55 minutes, depending on the size of the
potatoes and the cooking technique employed. Check
that they are cooked by piercing the top of the foil
pack and into the potatoes with a fine metal skewer.
Empty the potatoes into a warmed serving dish,
sprinkle over the remaining herbs and the sesame
seeds and dot with the remaining butter.

Baked potatoes with toppings

Select nicely shaped, even-sized baking potatoes. The ingredients for the toppings need to be well mixed before they are added to the potatoes.

Serves 4

4 medium/large baking potatoes
groundnut or sesame oil
salt and freshly ground black pepper or
your choice of barbecue spice

Prepare the barbecue for grilling or 'Indirect heat' cooking, following the instructions on **page 12** or **14**.

Scrub the potatoes well, pat dry and prick deeply all over with a skewer or fork. Brush with oil. (I find it easier, when tackling several potatoes, to use my hands.) Season with salt and pepper or sprinkle generously with barbecue spice. Wrap the potatoes in foil or, if you like a crispy skin, leave the potatoes unwrapped.

Grill over medium to high heat, and turn the potatoes several times during cooking (a medium-size potato will take 45–60 minutes and a large one 60–70 minutes). Alternatively, bake the potatoes by the 'Indirect heat' method, perhaps alongside a joint of meat that you are cooking. This will however take longer and it is a good idea to turn the potatoes over roughly halfway through cooking to avoid the top of the potato turning into 'parchment'.

Cut a cross in the top of each potato and pinch to open out the centre. Top with any of the suggested toppings or, better still, one of your own creation.

TOPPINGS:

Poor man's caviar with soured cream
4 teaspoons black or red lumpfish roe
150ml (^{1}/$_4$ pint) soured cream
1 tablespoon chopped fresh chives
a small pinch of cayenne pepper

Cream cheese and crispy bacon
125g (4oz) cream cheese or grated
Cheddar cheese
175g (6oz) crisply grilled back bacon,
crumbled
50g (2oz) butter
2 tablespoons finely chopped fresh chives
2 teaspoons finely chopped red pepper,
to garnish

Avocado and cheese
1 ripe medium avocado, roughly chopped
125g (4oz) cream cheese
freshly ground black pepper

Orange & ginger glazed carrots

The orange juice and ginger, combined with the butter or honey, makes an attractive and tasty glaze which combines well with the flavour of carrot. For a more piquant taste, replace the ginger with Worcestershire sauce.

Serves 4–6

1kg (2 lb) new carrots
2 oranges
2 teaspoons freshly grated root ginger
75g (3oz) butter or 2 tablespoons clear honey

Parboil the carrots in boiling, lightly salted water until barely tender, but still crisp. Drain well. Grate the zest from the oranges. Squeeze out and strain the juice.

Prepare the barbecue for grilling, following the instructions on **page 12**.

Combine the orange zest, orange juice, ginger, and butter or honey in a saucepan and, stirring constantly, bring the mixture to the boil. Simmer gently for about 5 minutes.

Dip the carrots in the mixture, coating them completely. Grill over medium heat for about 5 minutes, regularly turning and basting the carrots with the remaining sauce. If using the honey glaze, turn the carrots more frequently to avoid excessive caramelisation.

Tomatoes provençale

These make a fresh-tasting accompaniment to most grilled fish and meats. (Pictured on page 45.)

Serves 4–6

4 tablespoons softened butter
2 tablespoons finely chopped shallots
2 tablespoons chopped fresh parsley
$1/2$ teaspoon dried tarragon
a pinch of dried basil
$1/2$ teaspoon sugar
3 tablespoons dry white wine
4 medium tomatoes, peeled and quartered
2 garlic cloves, very finely chopped
salt and freshly ground black pepper

Prepare the barbecue for grilling, following the instructions on **page 12**.

Melt 2 tablespoons of the butter in a large skillet or heavy-based frying pan over high heat. Add the shallots, parsley, tarragon, basil, sugar and wine. Bring the mixture to the boil, stirring occasionally.

Add the tomatoes and stir gently until they are heated through. Add the remaining butter and the garlic and stir gently until the butter has melted. Remove immediately from the heat, season with salt and pepper and serve.

Sweetcorn with dill

Serves 6

6 young sweetcorn cobs, in their husks
125g (4oz) butter, softened
1 teaspoon dill weed
6 coriander seeds, crushed
1 teaspoon salt
a pinch of grated nutmeg

Loosen the husks sufficiently to strip away the silk. Soak the cobs in iced water for at least 30 minutes. When ready to cook, drain well.

Prepare the barbecue for grilling, following the instructions on **page 12**.

Blend together all the remaining ingredients and spread generously over the sweetcorn. Re-position the husks, place each cob on a sheet of foil and wrap securely. Grill over medium heat for 15–20 minutes, turning several times.

Bacon-wrapped corn

Serves 6

6 young sweetcorn cobs
1 quantity of Garlic butter or Tabasco & lemon butter (see pages 163 and 164), softened
6 rashers of streaky bacon, rinds removed

Remove the husks and silk and soak the cobs for 30 minutes in lightly salted, iced water. Soak 12 wooden cocktail sticks in water. When ready to cook, drain the cobs well.

Prepare the barbecue for grilling, following the instructions on **page 12**.

Spread the cobs generously with the flavoured butter. Wrap a rasher of bacon around the length of each cob and secure with 2 cocktail sticks. Grill over medium heat for about 25 minutes, turning frequently and basting any uncovered areas of the cobs with the butter, until the bacon is crisp and the uncovered corn is golden brown.

Roasted red peppers

Serves 4

4 large red peppers, de-seeded and cut in half
through the stalk, leaving the stalk intact
90ml (3fl oz) extra virgin olive oil, plus extra
for greasing
4 medium to large tomatoes
8 anchovy fillets, drained and each chopped into
4 pieces
2 large garlic cloves, finely sliced
freshly ground black pepper

Prepare the barbecue for 'Indirect heat' cooking,
following the instructions on **page 14**.

Lay the pepper halves, cut sides up, in an oiled
roasting tin. Place the tomatoes in a bowl and pour
boiling water over them. After a minute or so, having
drained away the water, it should be quite easy to
remove the skins from the tomatoes (use a cloth or
doubled kitchen paper to protect your hands). Cut the
tomatoes into quarters and place 2 quarters in each
half pepper to be joined by 4 anchovy pieces, plus a
few slices of garlic. Drizzle 2 teaspoons of the oil over
each pepper and season to taste with pepper.

Position the tin on the barbecue and cook with
medium to high heat for 45 minutes to 1 hour, until
the peppers have browned around their edges.

Transfer the cooked peppers to a shallow serving dish
and pour over all the juices from the tin.

If serving the roasted peppers as an appetiser, offer
your guests a basket of fresh bread chunks to dunk in
the delicious juices. Focaccia bread (see page 150)
happens to be my favourite 'blotting paper' for this
exercise.

Spicy nut roast

A delicious recipe that, although produced with the
vegetarian in mind, will appeal equally to the taste of
many members of the barbecuing carnivora. When
cold, it goes well with a salad.

Serves 4

1 tablespoon olive oil, plus extra for greasing
2 medium onions, finely chopped
1 large or 2 small green peppers, de-seeded
and finely chopped
50g (2oz) pecans, finely chopped
175g (6oz) walnut halves, finely chopped
75g (3oz) fresh breadcrumbs, preferably wholemeal
1 teaspoon each chopped fresh thyme and chopped
fresh parsley, or 1 teaspoon dried mixed herbs
1 garlic clove, very finely chopped
1 tablespoon mild or hot curry powder,
depending on taste
250g (8oz) firm ripe tomatoes, skinned and chopped
1 egg, beaten
salt and freshly ground black pepper

Prepare the barbecue for 'Indirect heat' cooking,
following the instructions on **page 14**.

Heat the oil in a pan, add the onions and peppers and
gently fry for about 10 minutes, or until they are soft.

Meanwhile, combine the nuts and breadcrumbs
together in a large bowl. Add the herbs, garlic, curry
powder and salt and pepper. Stir the onion and pepper
mixture, tomatoes and egg into the nut mixture. Bind
all together. Spoon the mixture into a greased 18cm
(7 inch) square cake tin, or the equivalent in an
ovenproof dish.

Bake, with medium heat, for 30–45 minutes until
golden brown.

Mixed vegetable kebabs

You may prefer to concentrate on one vegetable per skewer although, by so doing, the small interchange of flavours created by different vegetables nestling cheek by jowl will be lost.

Serves 6

6 very small potatoes, preferably new
6 small onions or shallots
12 small closed-cap mushrooms
1 large green pepper, de-seeded
2 small courgettes
50g (2oz) butter, melted
$1/2$ teaspoon garlic salt
$1/4$ teaspoon freshly ground black pepper
6 very small, firm tomatoes
oil for greasing skewers

Prepare the barbecue for grilling, following the instructions on **page 12**.

Cook the potatoes and onions separately in lightly salted, boiling water until they are barely tender.

Discard the stalks from the mushrooms and wipe the caps. Cut the pepper into 6 pieces. Cut the courgettes into 6 pieces, 2.5–4cm (1–1$1/2$ inches) long. Drain the onions and potatoes, and thread all but the tomatoes alternately on to 6 oiled metal (preferably flat-bladed) skewers.

Blend together the melted butter, garlic salt and pepper and brush the kebabs generously with the mixture.

Cook, turning frequently and basting with the butter, over medium to high heat, for about 5 minutes. Add a tomato to each skewer and continue cooking, turning and basting, for a further 5 minutes.

Gem squash McTaggart

Judy McTaggart, an old family friend, fell in love with this exotic vegetable during a photographic safari to Africa. A first-class cook, both indoors and outdoors, this is Judy's recipe for a vegetable that is readily available in supermarkets and greengrocers.

Serves 1–2

1 gem squash
50g (2oz) butter
salt and freshly ground black pepper

Prepare the barbecue for grilling or 'Indirect heat' cooking, following the instructions on **page 12** or **14**.

Remove the stem, and then cut the squash in half crossways and scoop out the seeds. Place half the butter in each half. Season lightly with salt and with a generous amount of pepper.

Place each half in the centre of a square of heavy-duty foil roughly 3 times the diameter of the vegetable. Bring the 4 corners of the foil together into a pyramid shape. Loosely fold over the foil edges, where they meet, to seal. Keep the package upright and grill, over high heat, for about 15 minutes; or bake – using the 'Indirect heat' method – for 25–30 minutes.

Helen Louise's fancy fried rice

Serves 2–3

3 eggs
2 tablespoons vegetable oil
1 medium onion, finely chopped
3 rashers of streaky bacon, cut into thin strips
25g (1oz) butter
375–500g ($^3/_4$–1 lb) cooked rice
3 tablespoons peas (fresh or frozen)
3 tablespoons peeled prawns (fresh or frozen), chopped
75–125g (3–4oz) bamboo shoots, very finely chopped (fresh asparagus can be substituted)
1 tablespoon soy sauce

Break the eggs into a bowl and beat for about 10 seconds, then put the bowl to one side.

Prepare the barbecue for wok-cooking, following the instructions on **page 19**.

Place the wok on the barbecue, heat the oil in it, then add the onion and stir-fry over high heat for about 2 minutes until the onion starts to soften. Add the bacon and continue stir-frying for another 2 minutes or until the bacon has crisped up. Remove the onion and bacon to a dish and keep warm adjacent to the barbecue. Add the butter to the wok. When melted, pour in the beaten egg and leave for about a minute or until just starting to set. At this point add the rice, peas, prawns, bamboo shoots, reserved onion and bacon and the soy sauce. Quickly and thoroughly stir and turn the fried rice mixture, from the bottom up, for 2–3 minutes. If you are using a gas barbecue, turn the heat down to a low setting for these final few minutes. Serve immediately.

Pilau rice

This highly spiced rice dish of Eastern origin goes well with most meats – particularly when grilled as kebabs. (Pictured on page 87.)

Serves 4

40g (1$^1/_2$ oz) butter
1 medium onion, finely chopped
175g (6oz) long-grain rice, washed and drained
450ml ($^3/_4$ pint) chicken stock or water
a pinch of saffron powder or turmeric
$^1/_2$ teaspoon dried oregano
salt and freshly ground black pepper

Prepare the barbecue for 'Indirect heat' cooking, following the instructions on **page 14**.

Melt the butter in an ovenproof baking dish. Add the onion and cook until soft and slightly brown. Add the rice and cook, over moderate heat, for 2–3 minutes.

Stir in the chicken stock or water, saffron powder or turmeric, oregano and salt and pepper to taste.

Cook, with low to medium heat, for 20–25 minutes or until all the liquid has been absorbed and the rice is fluffy and tender.

Saffron rice

Called *kesari chaval* in Hindi, this is a special rice dish that is traditionally served at Diwali – the festival of lights.

Serves 4

175g (6oz) basmati rice
a pinch of saffron threads
60 ml (2fl oz) hot water
$1^1/_2$ tablespoons olive oil
6 garlic cloves, very finely chopped
4 green cardamom pods, cracked
2.5 cm (1 inch) piece of cinnamon stick
$^1/_2$ teaspoon salt
20 whole almonds, blanched
75g (3oz) golden raisins

Prepare the barbecue for 'Indirect heat' cooking, following the instructions on **page 14**.

In a bowl, cover the rice with warm water. Allow to soak for 30 minutes before straining.

In a small bowl, soak the saffron in the hot water for about 20 minutes.

In a medium pan, heat the oil over high heat until it is very hot – but not smoking. Add the garlic, cardamom pods and cinnamon stick and cook, stirring constantly, for about 30 seconds or until the cardamom begins to 'pop'.

Stir in the rice, salt, raisins, almonds, 450ml ($^3/_4$ pint) cold water and the saffron, together with its soaking liquid, and bring to the boil. Cover the saucepan, and place in position on the barbecue. Cook with just enough heat for simmering to take place for about 15 minutes, or until the rice is light and fluffy and cooked through.

Serve immediately.

Tomato & onion salad

This can be eaten as a tasty and refreshing starter, especially when served with some crusty French bread. (Pictured on page 109.)

Serves 4

4 large or 6 small firm, ripe tomatoes, skinned and thinly sliced
2 medium onions, thinly sliced and separated into rings
1 teaspoon torn fresh basil leaves
2 tablespoons chopped fresh parsley
1 quantity of Vinaigrette dressing (see page 130)

Arrange the tomato slices on a large flat plate. Try not to overlap them if you prepare the salad more than an hour before it is eaten because this tends to make the slices soggy. Scatter the onion rings over the tomatoes. Sprinkle with the herbs and drizzle over the dressing.

Aubergine & pepper salad

Serves 4

A simple, tasty and colourful salad originating in Catalonia where a wood fire would have been used instead of a newfangled barbecue, but the end results are selfsame.

2 aubergines
2 red peppers
4 tablespoons olive oil
3 tablespoons torn fresh basil leaves
1 fat garlic clove, finely chopped
salt

Prepare the barbecue for grilling, following the instructions on **page 12**.

Place the aubergines and peppers on the grill and cook, turning frequently, for 15 minutes or until the skins are charred and the flesh feels soft.

As soon as they have cooled enough to handle, remove the skins and split in half lengthways. Remove the seeds from the peppers and cut the aubergine and pepper segments into long strips. Arrange the strips on a serving dish and season to taste with the oil and salt. Sprinkle with the basil and garlic and serve.

Salade niçoise

Prepare the salad as close as possible to its serving time in order to keep the lettuce fresh and crisp.

Serves 4–6

1 firm round lettuce
3 firm tomatoes, skinned, de-seeded and quartered
$1/2$ small cucumber, peeled and cut into small chunks
1 medium-size red pepper, de-seeded and cut into narrow strips
2 spring onions, finely chopped
125g (4oz) French beans, blanched in boiling water for 1 minute
2 hard-boiled eggs, quartered
50g (2oz) black olives, stoned
200g (7oz) can of tuna, drained and broken into chunks
6 anchovy fillets, drained and halved lengthways
2 teaspoons capers (optional)

For the vinaigrette dressing:
1 garlic clove, crushed
1 teaspoon sea salt
1 teaspoon mustard powder
1 tablespoon red or white wine vinegar
a pinch of freshly ground black pepper
6 tablespoons extra virgin olive oil
1 tablespoon chopped fresh tarragon (optional)

First make the dressing. Using a pestle and mortar, pound the garlic with the salt until you have a smooth paste. Add the mustard powder, vinegar and pepper and mix thoroughly until the salt has completely dissolved. Add the oil and tarragon (if using). Pour the vinaigrette into a screw-top jar and, just before dressing the salad, give it a good shake to blend all the ingredients thoroughly.

Shake the lettuce dry. Remove the outer leaves and arrange around the base of a large salad bowl. Cut the heart into quarters and place on the base of the bowl. Sprinkle over a little of the dressing. Arrange the tomato quarters and cucumber pieces in layers over the lettuce with a little more dressing; then add the pepper strips, spring onions, and French beans. Top with the hard-boiled eggs, olives and tuna. Scatter over the strips of anchovy fillet and the capers (if using). Spoon over more of the dressing and serve.

Caesar salad

Sometimes described as the classic American salad, this goes well with most barbecued food.

Serves 4

3 tablespoons lemon juice
2 tablespoons olive oil
2 tablespoons red wine vinegar
1 tablespoon Worcestershire sauce
4 garlic cloves, crushed
6 slices of white bread, crusts removed,
cut into 1cm ($1/2$ inch) cubes
50g (2oz) butter
1 Cos lettuce
1 egg, beaten well or parboiled in its shell for
2 minutes
50g (2oz) Roquefort or blue cheese, crumbled
50g (2oz) anchovy fillets, drained and cut
lengthways into strips (optional)
salt and freshly ground black pepper

In a jug mix together the lemon juice, oil, vinegar, Worcestershire sauce and half the crushed garlic. Allow to stand for 4–6 hours. Strain to remove the garlic.

Toast the bread cubes on a baking sheet in a pre-heated moderately hot oven or on a pre-heated barbecue, stirring them occasionally until the cubes are lightly browned on all sides. Melt the butter in a large frying pan, add the remaining garlic and the toasted bread cubes and stir continuously until the cubes have absorbed the butter and are golden.

Separate the lettuce leaves, tearing the largest ones in half with your hands. Place the leaves in a large salad bowl. Pour the beaten or parboiled egg over the lettuce and add the dressing. Toss well until all traces of the egg disappear.

Add the crumbled cheese, anchovy fillets (if using) and bread cubes. Season to taste with salt and pepper and toss again.

Brown rice & vegetable salad

Serves 6–8

1 tablespoon groundnut oil
300g (10oz) brown rice
600ml (1 pint) boiling water
4 tablespoons Vinaigrette dressing (see Salade niçoise, opposite)
2 large tomatoes, cut into thin wedges
$1/2$ red or green pepper, de-seeded and finely chopped
5cm (2 inch) piece of cucumber, finely chopped
1 red medium dessert apple, cored and chopped
1 small celery stick, finely chopped
2 tablespoons finely chopped spring onion or onion
25g (1oz) walnuts, finely chopped
25g (1oz) currants
salt and freshly ground black pepper

Heat the oil in a pan, add the rice and stir to coat all the grains. Add about 1 teaspoon of salt, pour over the boiling water and bring back to the boil. Stir once only, cover and simmer gently for 40 minutes or until all the liquid has been absorbed and the rice is bite-tender.

Tip the rice into a salad bowl and fluff it with a fork. Pour the dressing over whilst the rice is still warm. Allow to cool.

When the rice is cold, stir in all the other ingredients, adding a little more dressing if desired, and season to taste. Keep the salad in a cool place until required.

Bean sprout salad with koi-kuchi-shoyu dressing

A colourful and delicious salad. (*Koi-kuchi-shoyu* is the Japanese phrase for regular soy sauce.)

Serves 4

$1/4$ teaspoon salt
125g (4oz) carrot, cut into matchsticks
250g (8oz) bean sprouts
2 small green peppers, quartered, de-seeded and cut into matchsticks
1 small red pepper, quartered, de-seeded and cut into matchsticks
2 teaspoons sesame seeds, toasted (optional)

For the dressing:
3 tablespoons soy sauce
1 tablespoon olive or groundnut oil
2 tablespoons red wine vinegar
1 tablespoon sesame oil

First make the dressing by shaking all the ingredients together in a screw-top jar.

Bring 300ml ($1/2$ pint) of water to the boil. Add the salt and the carrot strips and blanch for 1 minute. Add the bean sprouts and peppers and, when the water simmers again, remove the pan from the heat. Drain off the water through a colander, compress the vegetables lightly to remove excess water and fan vigorously for 2–3 minutes to cool quickly.

Tip the salad into a large bowl, add the dressing and mix together gently.

Serve the salad in small individual bowls, leaving guests to sprinkle with the sesame seeds if desired.

Oriental cucumber & radish salad

Serves 4

12 fat radishes
1 small cucumber

For the dressing:
$1^1/2$ tablespoons soy sauce
$1/2$ tablespoon red wine vinegar
2 teaspoons sesame oil
$1/2$ teaspoon sugar

Cut the tops off the radishes. Crush each radish to open it up whilst keeping it intact (use the side of a broad-bladed knife, or cleaver, for this task).

Cut the cucumber into pieces approximately 5cm (2 inches) long and gently crush. Cut the crushed cucumber lengthways into halves or quarters.

Combine all the ingredients for the dressing and mix well.

Arrange the radishes and cucumber pieces on a plate, pour over the dressing and serve.

Potato salad

Serves 4–6

1kg (2 lb) waxy potatoes with their skins on
$1/2$ teaspoon mustard powder
4 spring onions, finely chopped
150ml ($1/4$ pint) mayonnaise (see following recipe)
2 tablespoons chopped fresh parsley
paprika, for sprinkling
salt and freshly ground black pepper

Boil or steam the potatoes in their skins until just tender. Drain, peel and dice them.

Mix the mustard and spring onions into the mayonnaise and add salt and pepper to taste.

Add the mayonnaise to the potatoes and mix gently with a spoon until they are well coated – this process is easier if the potatoes are still warm. Taste and adjust the seasoning if necessary. Sprinkle with the parsley and a little paprika.

Mayonnaise

It is essential that the oil, egg yolk and wine vinegar are at normal (cool rather than warm) room temperature.

Makes about 150ml ($1/4$ pint)

1 egg yolk
$1/4$ teaspoon salt
$1/2$ teaspoon mustard powder
a pinch of freshly ground white pepper
150ml ($1/4$ pint) olive or vegetable oil
1 tablespoon white wine vinegar or lemon juice

Place the egg yolk in a bowl and very gradually beat in the salt, mustard and pepper. A wire balloon whisk is probably the best tool for this job; or use a small hand mixer or wooden spoon.

Add the oil, drop by drop, whisking vigorously after each addition. Once the mixture forms a shiny emulsion and has become thick (roughly half the oil will have been used), the oil can be added more quickly, say, 1 tablespoon at a time.

When the mixture is very thick, add the wine vinegar or lemon juice and mix in. Then blend in the remaining oil. The finished consistency should be similar to lightly whipped double cream. Taste and adjust the seasoning to your liking.

The mayonnaise can be stored in the refrigerator, in a covered container, for up to 2 weeks.

 Note: If you prefer to use a blender to make the mayonnaise, use a whole egg and add the oil in a thin stream with the blender set at a moderate speed.

fruit & puddings

Spiced peaches; Barbados oranges; Pam & Ron's famous stuffed pears; Aunt Julia's apple slices, Grilled grapefruit; Norman's 'naughty but nice' pineapple flambé; Mixed fruit & bread kebabs; Cinnamon-stuffed apples; Martin's boozy pineapple; Rum chocolate banana split; Honey, nutmeg & cinnamon-basted nectarines; Gateau paysanne; Barbecued bread & butter pudding; Apple pie; Individual chocolate puddings with a hot chocolate sauce; Aran rice pudding.

Spiced peaches

Spiced peaches are delicious served as a dessert with cream or yoghurt but they also go well with ham, pork and poultry.

Serves 4

5 ripe, firm peaches
50g (2oz) soft brown sugar
1 tablespoon Worcestershire sauce
a pinch of ground cinnamon
a pinch of ground ginger

Halve and stone the peaches.

Place the sugar, Worcestershire sauce, cinnamon and ginger in a saucepan and heat very gently until the sugar has dissolved. Arrange the peach halves in a shallow foil tray and spoon the sugar mixture over them. Leave the peaches for 2–3 hours, turning them occasionally.

Prepare the barbecue for grilling, following the instructions on **page 12**.

Lightly drain the peaches and grill, over medium heat, until they are just heated through and beginning to brown.

Barbados oranges

As an alternative to rum, the equivalent amount of kirsch liqueur would do very nicely.

Serves 1

1 ripe orange, preferably seedless
1 tablespoon soft brown sugar
a pinch of ground cinnamon
1 tablespoon rum
1 tablespoon softened butter or margarine

Prepare the barbecue for grilling, following the instructions on **page 12**.

Peel the orange, removing pips if necessary, and carefully separate into segments. Place the segments on a piece of doubled foil. Sprinkle over the sugar, cinnamon and rum. Dot the segments with the butter or margarine before wrapping the edges of the foil together securely.

Place the package on the grill and cook, over medium heat, for 15–20 minutes. Serve topped with whipped cream or vanilla ice cream.

Pam & Ron's famous stuffed pears

This recipe, one of my all-time favourites, was borrowed from Pam and Ron Heath, great friends whose culinary skills I have long envied, admired and often sampled.

Serves 6

6 ripe, firm Comice pears, stalks intact
juice of 2 lemons
butter for greasing
caster sugar for dusting

For the almond stuffing:
50g (2oz) unsalted butter
25g (1oz) caster sugar
25g (1oz) ground almonds
grated zest of 1 lemon
25g (1oz) glacé cherries, finely chopped
a pinch of ground cinnamon
a pinch of ground ginger
1 teaspoon kirsch

For the stuffing, cream together the butter and sugar. Add the ground almonds, lemon zest, glacé cherries, cinnamon, ginger and kirsch and mix well.

Lightly trim the base of the pears so they can stand upright. Thinly peel the pears, taking care to leave the stalks intact. Put the lemon juice in a saucer. Stand each pear in the saucer and brush liberally all over with the juice. Cut the top off each pear about 2.5cm (1 inch) below the base of the stalk and reserve. Scoop out the pear cores, using a narrow sharp-pointed teaspoon, leaving about 1cm (^{1}/2 inch) of the flesh at the base intact. Take care not to break through the base of the pear.

Prepare the barbecue for grilling or 'Indirect heat' cooking, following the instructions on **page 12** or **14**.

Stuff the pear cavities with equal portions of the stuffing. Replace the pear tops and stand each pear on a lightly greased 25cm (10 inch) square of heavy-duty aluminium foil. Brush the remaining lemon juice over the pears and dust with caster sugar. Gather and twist the foil around the base of the stalks to secure. Stand the packaged pears in a shallow roasting tin or a double-thickness foil drip pan (see page 170).

Cook with medium heat, by the 'Indirect heat' method for about 45 minutes or grill the pears for about 30–35 minutes. The pears are ready when they feel soft when gently squeezed – take care not to overcook them. Handle the pears by the stalks.

The pears are at their luscious best when they have been given a few minutes to cool down a little. Serve with single, double or clotted cream, or vanilla ice cream.

Aunt Julia's apple slices

Serves 4

2 large apples, peeled, cored and cut into 2cm
($3/4$ inch) thick slices
2 tablespoons lemon juice
2 tablespoons white or soft brown sugar
1 tablespoon ground cinnamon
1 teaspoon ground ginger (optional)
40g (1$1/2$oz) butter, melted

Spread the apple slices over a large plate, sprinkle with the lemon juice and set aside for a few minutes. Drain off any liquid. Mix together the sugar and cinnamon, and ground ginger (if using).

In the meantime prepare the barbecue for grilling, following the instructions on **page 12**.

Brush some of the melted butter over the barbecue's griddle plate, or a large piece of doubled foil set on top of the grill, and place the slices in a single layer. Brush the slices with melted butter and lightly sprinkle with roughly half of the sugar mixture.

Cook, over medium to high heat, for 3–4 minutes. After turning the slices over, brush with the remaining butter, sprinkle lightly with the sugar mixture and cook for another 3–4 minutes, or until the slices are tender.

Serve immediately, allowing guests, if they wish, to sprinkle more of the sugar/cinnamon mixture over their helping.

Grilled grapefruit

A refreshing retro starter, entrée or dessert.

Serves 6

3 grapefruit
3 tablespoons clear honey or brown sugar
3 tablespoons sweet sherry (optional)
6 maraschino cherries

Prepare the barbecue for grilling or 'Indirect heat' cooking, following the instructions on **page 12** or **14**.

Slice each grapefruit in half, cut the segments loose and remove the pips.

Place each grapefruit half on a piece of doubled foil large enough to enclose the fruit. Spoon over about half a tablespoon of the honey or sugar, and half a tablespoon of the sherry (if using). Put a cherry in the centre of each half before wrapping the edges of the foil together securely.

Place the packages on the grill and cook, over medium heat, for approximately 15 minutes.

Alternatively, omit the cherries, leave the packages open, with the edges turned up to contain the juices, and cook by the 'Indirect heat' method for 15–20 minutes. (By this method, the sugar or honey on top of the grapefruit caramelises.) Place the cherries on top when the cooking is completed.

Norman's 'naughty but nice' pineapple flambé

A sweet alternative use for the beverage that my friend Norman swears is best for keeping the blood in circulation, whilst standing up to one's thighs (occasionally armpits!) in the chilly waters of a salmon river.

Serves 4

1 ripe pineapple or 8 whole slices of canned pineapple
7 tablespoons clear runny honey
3 tablespoons white rum
clotted cream or vanilla ice cream, to serve

If using a fresh pineapple, slice off the skin and cut out the fibrous centre, if liked. Cut the pineapple crossways into 8 slices.

Prepare the barbecue for grilling, following the instructions on **page 12**.

Grill the pineapple slices over high heat for 2–3 minutes on each side whilst brushing frequently with the honey.

Place the hot pineapple slices on a serving dish and sprinkle over the rum. Set the rum alight and serve immediately with clotted cream or vanilla ice cream.

Mixed fruit & bread kebabs

A beautiful and colourful composition that is particularly appropriate for 'special' barbecue parties. Take my tip and make up an extra skewer or three that consist solely of bread cubes – as you will discover, they are exceedingly 'moreish' (extra butter and caster sugar will be required if you do so).

Serves 6

2 ripe, firm pears, peeled and cored
1 small melon, chopped into bite-size pieces
juice of 2 lemons
2 oranges, cut into 1cm ($^1/_2$ inch) slices
1 small pineapple, peeled and cored,
or a 250g (8oz) can of pineapple chunks
12 large, firm strawberries
2 medium, firm bananas, each cut into 3
6 large, seedless grapes
125g (4oz) caster sugar, plus extra for dusting
3 tablespoons of your favourite liqueur
4 tablespoons white wine
1 white loaf, crusts removed
125g (4oz) butter, melted
oil for greasing skewers

Cut the pears into large chunks. Place them, together with the melon pieces and the lemon juice, in a large bowl. Quarter each orange slice and cut the fresh pineapple, if using, into 2.5cm (1 inch) cubes.

Place the orange pieces, fresh or canned pineapple chunks, strawberries, bananas and grapes in the bowl and add half the sugar, your chosen liqueur and the wine. Mix gently with your hands and leave the fruit to macerate in a cool place for 20–30 minutes. Prepare the barbecue for grilling, following the instructions on **page 12**.

Slice the bread into 2.5cm (1 inch) cubes and brush each, all over, with the melted butter. Toss the bread cubes in a bowl with the remaining sugar and coat them evenly. For each kebab, thread a selection of the fruit, together with 2 pieces of bread, onto an oiled metal, preferably flat-bladed, skewer.

Grill over medium heat for about 5 minutes, turning and dusting with more sugar, until the kebabs are lightly caramelised. If liked, warm the remaining marinade and sprinkle it over the kebabs before serving.

Cinnamon-stuffed apples

If you are not keen on cinnamon, try substituting 2 tablespoons rum (or a little rum flavouring if the stuffed apples are for children's consumption).

Serves 6

6 medium cooking apples, cored
125g (4oz) soft brown sugar
2 teaspoons ground cinnamon
a pinch of ground cloves
40g (1½oz) walnuts, finely chopped
40g (1½oz) raisins, finely chopped
1 tablespoon lemon juice
6 teaspoons soft butter

Prepare the barbecue for grilling, following the instructions on **page 12**.

Place each apple on a piece of doubled foil about 20cm (8 inches) square. Combine the sugar, cinnamon, cloves, walnuts, raisins and lemon juice and use to fill the centres of the apples. Top each apple with 1 teaspoon of the butter. Bring the edges of the foil up to enclose the apples securely.

Grill the wrapped apples over medium heat for 40–50 minutes, or until the apples feel soft when pressed.

Serve topped with whipped cream or ice cream.

Martin's boozy pineapple

My old pal Martin Cobban is the complete barbecue buff and a leading member of the British Barbecue Brigade. This, apparently, is his favourite barbecue recipe. I wonder why?

Serves 4–6

1 ripe pineapple
2 glasses kirsch
200ml (7fl oz) crème fraîche, to serve

Slice the top 2.5cm (1 inch) off the pineapple, and put it to one side.

Using a tablespoon, scoop out and reserve about 4cm (1½ inches) of pineapple flesh. Pour 1 glass of the kirsch into the cavity. Having drunk the remaining glass, replace the pineapple's top.

Prepare the barbecue for 'Indirect heat' cooking, following the instructions on **page 14**.

Place the booze-laden pineapple on the barbecue and cook, with medium heat, for about 35 minutes.

Discarding the 'lid', cut the pineapple into 1cm (½ inch) slices and serve with the reserved pineapple flesh and a spoonful of crème fraîche.

Rum chocolate banana split

A dish that requires a steady hand, time to spare and sweet-toothed guests in the two to ninety-two age group.

Serves 1 (just about)

1 large, medium-ripe, firm banana
1 teaspoon lemon juice
1 teaspoon rum or a few drops of rum flavouring
25g (1oz) good-quality dark chocolate, roughly chopped
2 marshmallows, each cut into 8 pieces

Peel the banana and place on the centre of a piece of heavy-duty foil (or use a double thickness of ordinary foil) about 23 x 15cm (9 x 6 inches) in size. Sprinkle the lemon juice over the banana so that it drains down onto the foil.

Using a small-bladed knife, carefully cut a V-shaped wedge from the banana along its length. Put the wedge to one side. The cavity should be roughly 1cm ($1/2$ inch) wide and 1cm ($1/2$ inch) deep.

Sprinkle the rum or rum flavouring into the cavity. Partially fill the cavity with the chocolate and top with the marshmallow pieces. Press the banana wedge firmly back into place. Lap the long edges of the foil together, leaving a small air space. Firmly squeeze the open ends of the package and turn the crushed ends upwards so that the package is roughly gondola-shaped. Chill the package in the refrigerator until required, keeping the 'boat' upright.

Prepare the barbecue for grilling, following the instructions on **page 12**.

Place the package on the grill and cook over medium heat for about 10 minutes or until the chocolate softens. If cooking lots of bananas, check the progress of one of the packages situated on or near the barbecue's 'hot spot' (see 'Tricks of the trade', page 178) after 5–6 minutes. Overcooking will make the flesh of the banana pulpy and perhaps result in the banana subsiding into an unattractive splodge.

Serve with whipped cream or vanilla ice cream. For the children, shake over some chocolate vermicelli.

Honey, nutmeg & cinnamon-basted nectarines

Serves 2

2 ripe medium nectarines, halved and stoned
2 tablespoons runny honey
1 tablespoon butter, melted
$1/8$ teaspoon freshly grated nutmeg
$1/8$ teaspoon cinnamon

Prepare the barbecue for grilling, following the instructions on **page 12**.

Arrange the nectarine halves in a shallow foil tray and brush all over with the melted butter. Cook for 10–12 minutes, occasionally brushing the cut surfaces and cavities with the honey.

Sprinkle over with the nutmeg and cinnamon and serve whilst the nectarines are still warm.

Gateau paysanne

This traditional French pudding originated in Normandy. Based on dessert apples, it is a batter pudding, rather like a clafoutis. It is best served just warm and needs no last-minute attention. I have cooked it on numerous occasions at my barbecue cookery demonstrations where it has proved immensely popular with stand staff and visitors alike. Like the wonderful Bread & butter pudding (see page 144) it is one of those puddings that has everyone scrapping to scrape off the crusty little bits left over in the dish.

You will require a flameproof dish measuring about 20 x 20 x 5cm deep (8 x 8 x 2 inches) or one holding approximately 1.75 litres (3 pints).

Serves 6–8

750g (1¹/₂ lb) dessert apples, peeled, cored, quartered and thinly sliced
175g (6oz) caster sugar, plus extra for sprinkling (optional)
2 eggs
200ml (7fl oz) crème fraîche (this gives the pud a certain je ne sais quoi)
50g (2oz) plain flour
50g (2oz) currants
75g (3oz) butter, plus extra for greasing
icing sugar for sprinkling (optional)

Grease the dish with butter. In a bowl, whisk the sugar with the eggs, then blend in the crème fraîche and flour to make a smooth batter. Spoon about a third of this batter into a cup and reserve. Mix the apple slices and currants with the larger quantity of batter. Pour the mixture into the buttered dish and level roughly with the back of a spoon. Try to leave several apple pieces sticking up to burn or caramelise as this will enhance the appearance of the dish.

Prepare the barbecue for 'Indirect heat' cooking, following the instructions on **page 14**.

Place the dish on the barbecue and bake for about 15 minutes. Allow an extra few minutes if the air temperature is low. Meanwhile, melt the butter and mix it thoroughly with the reserved batter. Pour the butter-batter mix over the apple-batter mixture and return the dish to the barbecue for a further 15–20 minutes, or until the top of the pudding is golden brown. Remove from the barbecue and allow to cool for several minutes.

Sprinkle with caster or icing sugar (if using) and serve with single cream, clotted cream or vanilla ice cream.

Barbecued bread & butter pudding

I am an associate member of the BBABPA (British Bread and Butter Pudding Association) whose prime aim is to promote this quintessential British pud to the world at large. Roast beef and Yorkshire pudding, along with Cheddar cheese, and our superb strawberries and apples (to mention but a few) are recognised, and rightly revered, by foreign gastronomes visiting our shores, but most return home woefully unaware of the above delicacy. Fortunately there are many oases in Great Britain where 'B & BP' appears regularly on the menu. I was lucky enough to sample a truly outstanding, five-star yummy specimen at celebrity chef Brian Turner's London restaurant a few years ago. The following 'naughty but nice' version is probably not one for calorie counters – but who cares?

Serves 4

softened butter for spreading and greasing
8 thin slices of bread cut from a small loaf
15g (1/2oz) candied lemon or orange peel, finely chopped
75g (3oz) currants
300ml (1/2 pint) milk
75ml (3fl oz) double cream
50g (2oz) caster sugar
1/4 teaspoon grated lemon zest
3 eggs, beaten
a little freshly grated nutmeg

Butter the bread. Grease a 1 litre (1 3/4 pint) oblong baking dish with butter.

Arrange 4 slices of the bread, butter side down, over the base of the dish. Sprinkle the candied peel and half the currants over the bread and cover with the remaining slices, butter side up, and the remaining currants.

Combine the milk and cream and stir in the sugar and lemon zest. Whisk the beaten eggs into the mixture and pour over the bread. Sprinkle over a little nutmeg and leave to stand for 30–50 minutes.

Prepare the barbecue for 'Indirect heat' cooking, following the instructions on **page 14**.

Position the dish on the barbecue and bake, with medium to high heat, for 30–40 minutes or until the pudding is set and the top is golden and crisp. Leave to rest for about 10 minutes before serving.

Apple pie

Serves about 6

For the shortcrust pastry:
250g (8oz) plain flour, plus extra for dusting
a pinch of salt
125g (4oz) butter or margarine, cut into small pieces
2–3 tablespoons cold water
milk for brushing
caster sugar for sprinkling

For the filling:
500g (1 lb) cooking apples and/or Cox's Orange
Pippin dessert apples, peeled, cored and thinly sliced
125g (4oz) brown or white sugar
grated zest of $1/2$ lemon
1–2 cloves (optional)

To make the pastry, sift the flour and salt into a large mixing bowl, add the butter or margarine and rub in until the mixture resembles fine breadcrumbs. Mix in enough cold water with a round-bladed or palette knife to make a stiff dough. Lightly press the pastry into a ball and leave, wrapped in foil or in a plastic bag, in the refrigerator for 30 minutes.

Dust a work surface with flour and roll out a little more than half the pastry to a circle about 25cm (10 inches) in diameter. Carefully lift the dough to line a 20cm (8 inch) pie dish.

Pile the sliced apples on top and sprinkle over the sugar, lemon zest and cloves (if using). Dampen the edge of the dough with a little cold water. Roll out the remaining dough and carefully lay it over the apples. Press the edges together to seal and trim them with a sharp knife. Flute the edges.

Prepare the barbecue for 'Indirect heat' cooking, following the instructions on page 14.

Brush the pastry with milk and lightly sprinkle with caster sugar. Make a small slit in the top of the pie to allow the steam to escape.

If using a gas barbecue, bake the pie at medium to high heat for 15 minutes and then reduce the temperature slightly to a low to medium heat and bake for a further 25 minutes or until the pastry is nicely browned. If using a charcoal-burning covered unit, bake the pie for about 35 minutes at medium to high heat (the heat indicator, if there is one, should register around 200°C/400°F). To test whether the pie is fully cooked, use a thin metal skewer to pierce, remove and check a piece of apple from below the steam slit.

Remove the pie from the barbecue, sprinkle lightly with more caster sugar and allow to rest for a few minutes before serving.

Individual chocolate puddings with a hot chocolate sauce

Serves 4

butter for greasing
125g (4oz) self-raising flour
1 rounded tablespoon cocoa powder
$1/2$ teaspoon baking powder
$1/4$ teaspoon bicarbonate of soda
50g (2oz) caster sugar
1 large egg, beaten
1 tablespoon golden syrup
100ml ($3^1/2$fl oz) milk
100ml ($3^1/2$fl oz) sunflower oil
2–3 drops vanilla extract

For the chocolate sauce:
75g (3oz) good-quality dark chocolate
25g (1oz) unsalted butter
200ml (7fl oz) double cream
225g (8oz) icing sugar

Grease 4 x 175ml (6fl oz) pudding moulds with butter.

Prepare the barbecue for 'Indirect heat' cooking, following the instructions on **page 14**.

Sift the flour, cocoa powder, baking powder, bicarbonate of soda and sugar into a mixing bowl. Pour in the beaten egg together with the golden syrup, milk, oil and vanilla extract. Beat to make a smooth batter.

Pour the mixture into the buttered moulds. Having positioned the moulds on a flat baking tray, place the tray on the barbecue. If using a gas barbecue, adjust the heat control knob to a position between low and medium (a heat indicator should show 150°C/300°F). Bake for about 30 minutes, until the puddings feel springy to the touch. If using a charcoal-burning unit, make a moderate heat fire-bed and bake for about 30 minutes or until the puddings feel springy to the touch.

To make the sauce, melt the chocolate, butter and cream together in a bowl set over a pan of hot water. Gradually add the icing sugar and beat until the mixture becomes glossy.

Unmould the puddings onto warmed dessert plates. Pour the chocolate sauce over the puddings and serve.

Aran rice pudding

A deliciously rich rice pudding – the skin (best part of the pud) caramelises to hide a creamy, gooey middle.

Serves 4–6

125g (4oz) short-grain rice, washed and drained
900ml ($1^1/2$ pints) milk or a mixture of half water and half evaporated milk
50g (2oz) butter, plus extra for greasing
2 eggs
grated zest of $1/2$ lemon
freshly grated nutmeg to sprinkle

Put the rice into a heavy-based saucepan, add the milk, or water and evaporated milk, and bring slowly to just below simmering. Allow to cook very gently for about 10 minutes or until the rice is barely tender.

Add the butter and sugar and stir until the sugar has completely dissolved. Remove the saucepan from the heat and allow the contents to cool for 2–3 minutes.

Grease a 1 litre ($1^3/4$ pint) flameproof dish with butter.

Prepare the barbecue for 'Indirect heat' cooking, following the instructions on **page 14**.

Beat the eggs and lemon zest together and stir into the rice. Pour the mixture into the dish and sprinkle the surface with grated nutmeg.

Bake, with low to medium heat, for about 35–40 minutes (adding a few more minutes to the cooking time will give the pudding a thicker, creamier consistency, but overcooking and/or using too high a heat may transform it into something akin to a rice shortcake!).

bread
& pizzas

Daily bread; Focaccia; Wholemeal rolls; Cheese & herb rolls; Pizza dough; Pizza with mozzarella & tomato; Singin' hinnie.

Daily bread

Surely there are few things that provide the cook with more satisfaction than the sight of freshly baked bread which they have personally conjured up. And its smell is the most evocative aroma that can pervade a kitchen. Why not, therefore, occasionally use your barbecue as an alfresco baker's oven and let your neighbours share the enjoyment?

Apart from trying your hand at baking a standard white loaf, there is nothing to stop you tackling the more fancy shapes such as cottage, bloomer or plait; or, indeed, using your yeast dough to bake the odd batch of sticky buns, light brioches or even burger buns.

Makes 2 loaves

425ml (13fl oz) lukewarm water
1 teaspoon sugar
1 sachet easy-blend yeast
750g (1^1/$_2$ lb) strong white flour, plus
extra for dusting
1 teaspoon salt
25g (1oz) lard, butter or margarine,
plus extra for greasing

Pour about a third of the lukewarm water into a bowl, then whisk in the sugar followed by the yeast. Leave in a warm place until frothy.

Meanwhile sift the flour and salt into a warm bowl and rub in the lard, butter or margarine.

When the yeast is ready, make a well in the centre of the flour and pour in the yeast liquid followed by the remainder of the lukewarm water.

Starting with a wooden spoon, then using your hands, work the batter into a spongy dough. Dust a work surface with flour and turn the dough out onto it. Knead well for 10 minutes or so until the dough has developed a smooth sheen.

Return the dough to the bowl, cover with a plastic bag or cling film, and leave in a warm, draught-free place for 1–1^1/$_2$ hours until the dough has roughly doubled in bulk.

Turn out onto a floured surface and knead lightly for 30 seconds or so to expel the air from the dough. Grease a 23 x 13 x 13cm (9 x 5 x 5 inch) loaf tin.

Make a loaf shape with the dough and place in the prepared tin. Cover the tin with a plastic bag or cling film (oiled on the underside to prevent the risen dough from sticking), and prove in a warm place for 20–30 minutes or until the dough rises just above the top of the tin.

Meanwhile prepare the barbecue for 'Indirect heat' cooking, following the instructions on **page 14**. If using a gas barbecue, and depending upon its BTU rating, 'oven' capacity and the prevailing weather conditions, adjust the control knob to a position between medium and high so that the heat indicator reads 220°C (425°F). If using a charcoal-burning barbecue create a normal fire, which should result in a similar cooking temperature.

Place the tin on the barbecue, and bake for 30–35 minutes until the loaf is well browned and shrinking slightly from the sides of the tin.

Tip the loaf out onto a rack and check that it is ready by tapping its bottom; it should sound hollow. If the loaf appears somewhat pale on its base and sides, return it (out of its tin) to the barbecue for a couple of minutes.

Focaccia

Goes well with summer salads, makes a great 'sponge' for mopping up juices and can be used for 'jaw-aching' sandwiches.

Makes 1 focaccia

500g (1 lb) strong white flour, plus
extra for dusting
1 teaspoon salt
1 teaspoon sugar
1 sachet easy-blend yeast
6 tablespoons extra virgin olive oil
about 250ml (8fl oz) lukewarm water
2 tablespoons sea salt, crushed
handful of fresh rosemary leaves

Mix the flour, salt, sugar and yeast in a bowl. Stir in 4 tablespoons of the oil and most of the water to make a firm dough (add more water if required).

Lightly dust a work surface with flour. Turn the dough out onto it and knead for 5–10 minutes until it is shiny, smooth and pliable. Place in a large, lightly oiled bowl and cover with a clean tea towel or cling film. Leave in a warm place (perhaps adjacent to the barbecue if it is lit) for about 40 minutes until the dough has roughly doubled in size.

In the meantime prepare the barbecue for 'Indirect heat' cooking, following the instructions on **page 14**.

Knock back the risen dough and roll it out to a rectangle about 30 x 20cm (12 x 8 inches) x 2cm (3/4 inch) deep. Grease a baking sheet or shallow baking tray with oil and dust with flour. Place the dough on the baking sheet or fit it into the baking tray. Return the prepared dough to a warm place and leave to rise for about 10 minutes.

Using the end of a wooden spoon handle or, Italian style, your little finger or index finger, make deep indentations over the entire surface of the dough.

Drizzle the remaining oil over the dough and scatter with the sea salt and rosemary. Very lightly spray the surface with water.

Bake in the barbecue, with moderate high heat (about 200°C/400°F on the heat indicator if there is one) for about 25 minutes.

The focaccia is best when served warm or at room temperature.

Wholemeal rolls

Cheese & herb rolls

Makes 12 rolls

1 teaspoon soft brown sugar
250ml (8fl oz) lukewarm water
25g (1oz) fresh yeast or 1 sachet easy-blend yeast
500 (1 lb) wholemeal flour, plus extra for dusting
1 teaspoon salt
50g (2oz) cracked wheat

Dissolve the sugar in a third of the lukewarm water and add the fresh or dried yeast. Mix well and leave in a warm place until frothy.

Mix the flour and salt in a bowl. Stir the yeast mixture into the flour, gradually add the remaining water and mix with your hands to make a smooth dough. Dust a work surface with flour. Knead the dough on the floured surface for about 5 minutes until it is elastic and no longer sticky.

Divide the dough into 12 pieces and shape into rolls. Dust a baking sheet with flour. Place the rolls, spaced apart, on the baking sheet. Leave to rise, covered with a damp tea towel, in a warm place for 1–1 1/2 hours or until nearly doubled in size.

Prepare the barbecue for 'Indirect heat' cooking, following the instructions on **page 14**. If using a gas barbecue, and depending upon its BTU rating, 'oven' capacity and prevailing weather conditions, adjust the heat control knob to a position between medium and high. The heat indicator should read 220°C (425°F). If using a charcoal-burning unit create a normal fire, which should result in a similar cooking temperature.

Sprinkle the rolls with the cracked wheat and place the baking sheet on the barbecue. Bake for 10–15 minutes or until the rolls are nicely browned.

Makes 8 rolls

175g (6oz) butter, softened
125g (4oz) blue cheese, crumbled, or grated Cheddar cheese
1 tablespoon finely chopped onion
1 1/2 tablespoons chopped fresh parsley
1 teaspoon chopped fresh rosemary leaves
handful of fresh basil leaves, torn
8 bread rolls, halved

Prepare the barbecue for grilling, following the instructions on **page 12**.

Cream together the butter and cheese and stir in the onion, parsley, rosemary and basil. Spread the mixture over the cut sides of each roll. Place the halves together and wrap each roll in foil. Place the rolls on the grill and heat through over medium to high heat for 12–15 minutes, turning once.

Pizza dough

Your covered barbecue may be miles away in resemblance to a pizzeria in a small Italian village, but the end result – smell, taste and bubbling surface, is not that far removed, aided by a little imagination, from the genuine article.

Makes 2 pizza bases, each serving 2–4

1 sachet easy-blend yeast
75–125ml (3–4fl oz) lukewarm water
250g (8oz) strong white flour or wholemeal flour, plus extra for dusting
1 teaspoon salt
1 egg, beaten
1 teaspoon olive oil

Mix the yeast with the water and leave in a warm place for 10 minutes or until frothy.

Sift the flour and salt together in a bowl. Pour in the yeast mixture and the beaten egg and mix, using one hand, to a scone-like dough that leaves the bowl clean, adding an extra drop or two of warm water if necessary.

Dust a work surface with flour. Transfer the dough to the floured surface and knead for about 10 minutes until it is smooth and elastic. Return the dough to the bowl and rub the surface with the oil. Cover the dough with a clean, damp cloth and leave in a warmish place for about an hour, or until it has doubled in size.

Knead the dough lightly for a few minutes. It is now ready to be shaped into pizza bases.

Pizza with mozzarella and tomato

Serves 2–4

$1/2$ quantity of pizza dough (see left)

For the tomato sauce:
2 tablespoons olive oil
1 medium-size Spanish onion, chopped
2 garlic cloves, crushed
2 x 425g (14oz) cans of Italian plum tomatoes
handful of fresh basil leaves, torn
1 bay leaf
salt and freshly ground black pepper

For the topping:
2 tablespoons olive oil
125g (4oz) mozzarella cheese, thinly sliced
50g (2oz) can of anchovy fillets, drained and roughly chopped
10 large black olives, stoned and halved
1 teaspoon dried oregano
1 tablespoon freshly grated Parmesan cheese

To make the sauce, heat the oil in a saucepan and fry the onion until soft and golden. Add the garlic, tomatoes, basil, bay leaf and salt and pepper to taste. Simmer over gentle heat for about 40 minutes or until the tomato mixture is thick. Remove the pan from the heat, discard the bay leaf and leave the sauce to cool.

Place the pizza dough in either 1 large, shallow pizza tin about 25cm (10 inches) square, or 2 small tins. The dough should line the bottom and sides of the tin(s).

To make the topping, first brush the dough with a little of the oil. Cover with the tomato sauce and lay the mozzarella over the surface. Arrange the anchovies and olives attractively and sprinkle over the oregano and Parmesan. Trickle the remaining oil over the top. Leave the pizza(s) for 15 minutes before baking.

continues on p. 154

Meanwhile prepare the barbecue for 'Indirect heat' cooking, following the instructions on **page 14**. If using a gas barbecue, and depending upon its BTU rating, 'oven' capacity and the prevailing weather conditions, adjust the control knob to a position between medium and high so that the heat indicator reads 220°C (425°F). If using a charcoal-burning barbecue create a normal fire, which should result in a similar cooking temperature.

Place the pizza(s) on the barbecue, and bake for 15 minutes. To check that the dough is fully baked, lift an edge with a fish slice and take a peek.

Serve the pizza(s) straight from the barbecue, or cool on a wire rack and enjoy as a delicious cold addition to a picnic meal.

Topping variations

Salami and mushroom topping

125g (4oz) salami or garlic sausage, cut into matchsticks
75g (3oz) mushrooms, thinly sliced
75g (3oz) tomatoes, thinly sliced
75g (3oz) mozzarella or Bel Paese cheese, thinly sliced
salt and freshly ground black pepper

Layer the salami or garlic sausage, mushrooms and tomatoes on top of the tomato sauce. Season with salt and pepper and cover with the cheese.

Smoked mozzarella and sun-dried tomatoes

175g (6oz) smoked mozzarella cheese, cut into 2.5cm (1 inch) cubes
150g (5oz) sun-dried tomatoes in oil, drained (reserve the oil) and roughly chopped
50g (2oz) mushrooms, thinly sliced
10 black olives, stoned and sliced
1 tablespoons capers, drained
2 tablespoons torn fresh basil leaves
salt and freshly ground black pepper

Scatter the mozzarella, sun-dried tomatoes, mushrooms, olives, capers and basil over the tomato sauce. Season with salt and pepper, then drizzle 1$\frac{1}{2}$ tablespoons of the reserved tomato oil over the top.

Singin' hinnie

This traditional recipe hails from the north-east region of England where the phrase 'hinnie' (honey) is an endearment used by menfolk when addressing their nearest and dearest. As for the 'singing' bit, this alludes to the sound made as the hinnie sizzles during cooking on the hot girdle (a flat iron baking plate with a curved handle). One could place a girdle, or thick-based frying pan, on the barbecue, but this recipe is formulated for units that incorporate a griddle plate.

Makes 1, feeds 4–8

375g (12oz) plain flour
$1/2$ teaspoon salt
scant $1/2$ teaspoon bicarbonate of soda
1 teaspoon cream of tartar
75g (3oz) lard, plus extra for greasing
125g (4oz) currants
about 200ml (7fl oz) milk

Sift the flour, salt, bicarbonate of soda and cream of tartar together.

Rub in the lard and add the currants. Mix to a soft dough with the milk. Turn the dough out onto a floured surface and roll out to into a round roughly 1cm ($1/2$ inch) thick.

Prepare the barbecue for grilling, following the instructions on **page 12**.

Carefully place the hinnie on the griddle plate and bake over a gentle to moderate heat for about 5 minutes on each side (both sides should be nicely brown). When turning the hinnie, I suggest you use a couple of fish slices to deposit it onto a large plate then, having covered it with a second plate, invert the plates and slide the hinnie back onto the griddle plate for further cooking.

Remove the hinnie and let it cool slightly before splitting it with a long-bladed bread knife. Serve hot (as you would a teacake) with lots of butter and jam.

marinades, sauces & butters

Marinades: Sherry-ginger marinade; Soy-lemon marinade; Soy-sake marinade; Teriyaki marinade; Honey-mint marinade; Marinade vin rouge.
Sauces: Rich mustard sauce; Salsa; Chimchurri sauce; Sweet & sour barbecue sauce; Jim's new universal sauce; Honey & mustard sauce; Rich Chinese sauce; Indonesian sauce; Jim's jammy-ginger sauce; Soy, orange & wine sauce; Lily's luxury tomato sauce.
Butters: Lime & dill butter; Mustard & onion butter; Lemon & parsley butter; Garlic butter (medium strength); Blue cheese butter; Herb & garlic butter; Tabasco & lemon butter; Maitre d'hotel butter; Orange & honey butter; Tarragon & parsley butter.

Marinades

The prime function of a marinade is to tenderise and enhance the flavour of cuts of meat. Like a skilful football manager, a good marinade can be instrumental in promoting a first division cut of meat into the Premier League. Needless to say, there can be no substitute for prime quality, so whenever possible buy meat of the best grade (not necessarily of the highest price). In that way you are more than halfway to ensuring the best results in your cookouts.

The acid in a marinade, be it lemon juice, wine vinegar, wine or pineapple juice, acts as a tenderising agent; the fat (butter, oil or margarine) gives moistness to very lean meat and helps to protect it from losing too much succulence when cooked over high heat.

If the marinade is acid, it is advisable to use a glass or china receptacle. If the meat is not fully covered by the marinade, it will be necessary to turn it occasionally. A good and easy way to turn food is to place both marinade and food in a strong plastic bag (or two just to be on the safe side), which is then tightly sealed. As an extra safeguard, place the sealed bag in a baking tin.

Some foods can be left to marinate in the refrigerator for over 24 hours, whilst others only require a fleeting 'kiss' – say, 15 or so minutes. However, if marinating the food overnight in the refrigerator, remember to remove it at least an hour before cooking so that it can return to room temperature.

Sherry-ginger marinade
Makes about 150ml (1/4 pint)

4 tablespoons sweet sherry
2 teaspoons ground ginger
3 tablespoons soy sauce
1 tablespoon lemon juice
1 tablespoon brown sugar
2 tablespoons oil
Tabasco, to taste (drop by drop)
salt and freshly ground pepper, to taste

Combine all the ingredients and mix well. Use to marinate chicken, beef and spare ribs.

Soy-lemon marinade
Makes about 300ml (1/2 pint)

6 tablespoons lemon juice
6 tablespoons soy sauce
4 tablespoons groundnut or sunflower oil
1 teaspoon sesame oil
1/2 teaspoon freshly ground black pepper
1 garlic clove, crushed
1 bay leaf

Combine all the ingredients and allow the mixture to stand for at least an hour before use.

Excellent for joints of beef which can be left in the marinade (a strong well-sealed plastic bag is ideal for holding both joint and marinade) for up to 3 days in the refrigerator. The meat should be turned frequently and be well drained before roasting.

Soy-sake marinade
Makes about 300ml (1/2 pint)

4 tablespoons soy sauce
4 tablespoons sake or dry sherry
3 tablespoons groundnut or sunflower oil
2 tablespoons clear honey
1 teaspoon freshly grated root ginger
1 garlic clove, thinly sliced

Combine all the ingredients and mix well. Use with red and white meats, and fish such as salmon.

Teriyaki marinade
Makes about 150ml (1/4 pint)

1 1/2 tablespoons clear honey
1 1/2 tablespoons groundnut or sunflower oil
4 tablespoons soy sauce
1 tablespoon red wine or red wine vinegar
1 teaspoon freshly grated root ginger
1 large garlic clove, crushed

Combine all the ingredients and mix well.

Use to marinate chicken, beef, spare ribs or fish. Meat will need to be marinated for 4–8 hours or overnight in the refrigerator – turn it occasionally. Fish only requires marinating for about 2–4 hours in the refrigerator. This also makes a superb basting sauce. Try using it with grilled salmon steaks.

Honey-mint marinade
Makes about 300ml (1/2 pint)

150ml (1/4 pint) dry white wine
4 tablespoons clear honey
1 teaspoon soy sauce
1 tablespoon chopped fresh mint
1 tablespoon red or white wine vinegar
1 garlic clove, crushed
1 teaspoon salt

Combine all the ingredients and mix until well blended. Allow to stand for at least an hour before use. Particularly suitable with lamb, but can be used for chicken. Allow the meat to marinate for 1–2 hours.

Marinade vin rouge
Makes about 450ml (3/4 pint)

300ml (1/2 pint) dry red wine
6 tablespoons groundnut or sunflower oil
50g (2oz) finely chopped spring onion
2 garlic cloves, crushed
1 teaspoon dried oregano
1 teaspoon salt
1/2 teaspoon freshly ground black pepper

Combine all the ingredients in a heavy-based saucepan and heat until the marinade starts to simmer. Remove from the heat immediately, cover the pan and leave for about 1 hour to cool. Use with beef or pork.

Sauces

The distinction between marinades and sauces can be somewhat blurred but, in general terms, a marinade is something that is applied to the food before cooking, and a sauce is something that is applied to the food during cooking and then consumed as part of the dish.

Sauces are best prepared in heavy-based saucepans and stirred with a wooden spoon. Most sauces, and certainly those incorporating sugar, honey or tomato, are best applied to the meat during the final 10 minutes or so of cooking. If they are applied too early there is the likelihood that the surface of the meat will become unduly burnt.

Rich mustard sauce
Makes about 250ml (8fl oz)

100ml (3fl oz) sour cream
2 tablespoons Mayonnaise (see page 133 or use good-quality shop-bought)
2 tablespoons mustard (Dijon or wholegrain)
salt and freshly ground black pepper

Combine all the ingredients. Serve with chicken or beef.

Salsa

2 tablespoons fresh coriander leaves, chopped
250g (8oz) ripe tomatoes, de-seeded and diced
1 small red onion, very finely chopped
juice of 1/2 lemon
salt and freshly ground black pepper, to taste

Mix the salsa ingredients together and season to taste. Set aside for the flavours to blend.

Chimchurri sauce

5 large ripe tomatoes
1 large onion
1 head garlic
1 green chilli
large handful of fresh coriander leaves
125ml (4fl oz) extra virgin olive oil
125ml (4fl oz) red wine vinegar
salt and freshly ground black pepper

Place the tomatoes in a bowl and cover with boiling water. Leave for 2 minutes before draining and slipping off the skins (protect your hands when doing this). Cut the tomatoes open and remove their pips. Peel the onion and the garlic cloves, de-seed the chilli and rinse the coriander under cold running water to remove any grit.

Finely chop all the prepared ingredients, either by hand or briefly in a food processor, and place in a bowl. Stir in the oil and vinegar and season to taste. Serve this fabulous sauce with any grilled meat or fish.

Sweet & sour barbecue sauce
Makes about 300ml (1/2 pint)

250ml (8fl oz) tomato ketchup
150ml (1/4 pint) orange marmalade or apricot jam
2 tablespoons lemon juice
1 teaspoon Worcestershire sauce
1 teaspoon soy sauce
1/2 teaspoon horseradish sauce
1/2 teaspoon salt
a pinch of freshly ground black pepper

Put all the ingredients in a heavy-based saucepan and heat until simmering. Serve with pork.

Jim's new universal sauce

This makes enough to reserve some for future home cookouts – or how about making up a fancy label and taking a jar to an away cookout in lieu of a bottle of wine or a 'six-pack'?

Makes about 1.2 litres (2 pints)

2 tablespoons groundnut oil
2 garlic cloves, crushed
2 small green peppers, de-seeded and finely chopped
2 small onions, finely chopped
125g (4oz) celery, finely chopped
1/2 teaspoon dried basil
1/2 teaspoon dried thyme
1/2 teaspoon ground cinnamon
1 teaspoon salt
2 dashes of Tabasco
1/2 tablespoon Worcestershire sauce
450ml (3/4 pint) tomato ketchup
6 tablespoons red or white wine vinegar
1 tablespoon 'liquid smoke' (optional)
juice of 1 lemon
1 teaspoon grated lemon zest

Heat the oil in a large heavy-based saucepan and add the garlic, green peppers, onions and celery. Cook, over medium heat, for about 5 minutes, stirring frequently. Add 300ml (1/2 pint) water and all the remaining ingredients, except the lemon juice and zest, and cook for a further 5 minutes or so.

Add the lemon juice and zest and simmer, over gentle heat, for about 30–40 minutes, stirring occasionally towards the end of cooking. Add a little more water if the sauce is too thick. Serve with chicken, pork, beef or fish.

Honey & mustard sauce
Makes about 250ml (8fl oz)

6 tablespoons clear honey
3 tablespoons English or French mustard
1/2 teaspoon horseradish sauce
1 tablespoon cornflour
3 tablespoons red wine vinegar
2 tablespoons lemon juice

Put all the ingredients in a heavy-based saucepan and cook over gentle heat, stirring continuously, until the mixture clears and thickens slightly. Serve with hamburgers, steaks and chops.

Rich Chinese sauce
Makes about 450ml (3/4 pint)

6 tablespoons soy sauce
4 tablespoons clear honey
1 tablespoon soft brown sugar
1/2 teaspoon curry powder
1/2 teaspoon ground ginger
1 large garlic clove, crushed
1/2 teaspoon salt
a pinch of freshly ground black pepper
3 tablespoons preserved ginger, drained well and finely chopped
6 tablespoons dry or medium-dry sherry or dry white wine

Combine the soy sauce, honey, sugar, curry powder, ground ginger, garlic, salt and pepper in a heavy-based saucepan and, over gentle heat, bring to the boil, stirring continuously.

Draw the pan to one side and stir in the preserved ginger and the sherry or wine. Reduce the heat and simmer for 5–10 minutes, stirring until the sauce thickens. Serve with chicken, pork or beef.

Sauces

Indonesian sauce
Makes about 300ml (1/2 pint)

1 tablespoon groundnut oil
4 tablespoons smooth peanut butter
150ml (1/4 pint) tomato ketchup
3 tablespoons Worcestershire sauce
garlic powder, to taste
1/4 teaspoon salt

Heat the oil in a heavy-based saucepan and add the peanut butter. Cook over gentle heat, stirring occasionally, until the peanut butter thickens and darkens slightly. Remove the pan from the heat immediately and stir in the tomato ketchup and Worcestershire sauce.

Season the sauce to taste with garlic powder and the salt. Allow to stand for 2 hours before use.

Re-heat the sauce gently and add a little water if the sauce is too thick. Serve with chicken and steaks. It can also be used to baste chicken.

Jim's jammy-ginger sauce
Makes about 350ml (12fl oz)

500g (1 lb) apricot jam
4 tablespoons dry white wine or white wine vinegar
2 tablespoons melted butter
1 tablespoon freshly grated root ginger
1/2 teaspoon salt

Combine all the ingredients in a heavy-based saucepan and heat until simmering, stirring occasionally. Serve with chicken and pork.

Soy, orange & wine sauce
Makes about 450ml (3/4 pint)

4 tablespoons soy sauce
6 tablespoons orange juice
6 tablespoons soft brown sugar
150ml (1/4 pint) dry white wine
1/2 teaspoon mustard powder
1/2 teaspoon ground ginger
2 dashes of Tabasco
2 shallots, finely chopped
a pinch of ground cinnamon
3 tablespoons water
2 teaspoons cornflour
salt and freshly ground black pepper

Combine all the ingredients, except the cornflour and salt and pepper, in a heavy-based saucepan and bring slowly to the boil, stirring continuously. Allow to simmer for about 5 minutes. Stir in the cornflour to thicken. Season to taste with salt and pepper. Serve with chicken and pork.

Lily's luxury tomato sauce
Makes about 250ml (8fl oz)

1 tablespoon extra virgin olive oil
15g (1/2oz) butter
1 medium onion, finely chopped
1 garlic clove, crushed
1 teaspoon dried mixed herbs
2 large ripe tomatoes, skinned and roughly chopped
125ml (4fl oz) tomato purée
2 teaspoons balsamic vinegar
salt and freshly ground black pepper

Heat the oil and butter in a heavy-based saucepan and add the onion, garlic and herbs. Cook for about 3 minutes or until the onion has softened. Stir in the tomatoes, tomato purée and balsamic vinegar and continue cooking for a further 4–5 minutes, stirring occasionally. Remove the pan from the heat and allow to cool. Place the sauce in a food processor and liquidise until smooth. Season to taste with salt and pepper. Serve warm or cold with hamburgers, sausages, steaks, chops and fish.

Butters

Flavoured butter can be made seven to ten days before use, as long as it is kept in the refrigerator in a covered dish. You can melt it and brush it onto the food, or place a piece on the 'second' side of meat during the final two minutes of cooking, and allow it to melt. Some of the butters also make tasty and economical sandwich spreads. The 'use with' suggestions are not to be treated as sacrosanct, so please mix and match as you see fit.

To prepare the following butters, beat the butter until soft; then add and thoroughly mix in the other ingredients. Using wet hands, shape the butter into a roll about 4cm (1^1/$_2$ inches) in diameter. Wrap gently in foil and chill well. Keep in the refrigerator until ready to serve. All the butters are suitable for freezing.

Lime & dill butter

1 teaspoon lime zest
2 teaspoons lime juice
^{1}/$_2$ teaspoon finely chopped fresh dill
^{1}/$_4$ teaspoon freshly grated root ginger
125g (4oz) butter

Use with seafood, poultry and vegetables.

Mustard & onion butter

2 tablespoons Dijon mustard
1 tablespoon finely chopped spring onion
1 garlic clove, very finely chopped
^{1}/$_4$ teaspoon freshly ground black pepper
a dash of Worcestershire sauce
125g (4oz) butter

Use with red meat and duck.

Lemon & parsley butter

2 tablespoons lemon juice
1 teaspoon finely grated lemon zest
1 tablespoon dry white wine (optional)
1 tablespoon finely chopped fresh parsley
125g (4oz) butter

Use with seafood, poultry and vegetables.

Garlic butter (medium strength)

1 garlic clove, very finely chopped
1^1/$_2$ tablespoons chopped fresh parsley
125g (4oz) butter

Use with seafood, red meat, vegetables and French bread.

Blue cheese butter

75g (3oz) blue cheese, finely crumbled
1/4 teaspoon paprika
1 garlic clove, very finely chopped
1 tablespoon finely chopped spring onion
125g (4oz) butter

Use with red meat (including hamburgers). It also makes an excellent filling for baked potatoes.

Herb & garlic butter

1/2 teaspoon dried tarragon or rosemary
1 tablespoon finely chopped fresh chives
1 tablespoon finely chopped fresh parsley
1 garlic clove, chopped very finely
1/4 teaspoon salt
a pinch of freshly ground black pepper
125g (4oz) butter

Use with poultry, seafood, vegetables and French bread.

Tabasco & lemon butter

2 teaspoons Tabasco
1/2 teaspoon lemon juice
a pinch of salt

Use with seafood and poultry.

Maitre d'hotel butter

2 teaspoons finely chopped fresh parsley
1/2 teaspoon salt
2 teaspoons lemon juice
1/4 teaspoon dried thyme
a pinch of freshly ground black pepper
125g (4oz) butter

Use with vegetables and fish, or as a baste for chicken.

Orange & honey butter

1 tablespoon fresh orange juice
1 tablespoon finely grated orange zest
1 tablespoon clear honey
2 teaspoons finely chopped fresh parsley
125g (4oz) butter

Use with lamb, duck, chicken and turkey.

Tarragon & parsley butter

1/4 teaspoon dried crushed tarragon
1 tablespoon finely chopped fresh parsley
1/2 teaspoon grated lemon zest
2 teaspoons lemon juice
1/4 teaspoon salt
125g (4oz) butter

Use with red meat, especially steaks.

guide to equipment

Guide to Equipment

Charcoal-burning barbecues

Charcoal and wood-fuelled barbecues can be roughly divided into two categories:

Portable and Improvised

These models are designed for use away from the home base by picnickers, backpackers, campers, caravanners and the like.

Disposable Barbecues

For those travelling light, economically priced disposable barbecues are the practical choice simply because of their compact size and light weight. Disposable units, normally available in 2–3 sizes, comprise a shallow foil tray housing a quantity of lumpwood charcoal (adequate to provide 20–30 minutes cooking time), a sheet of lighting paper and a grill made from a piece of expanded metal. These very handy little barbecues can be refuelled and placed in a carrier bag (to prevent the charcoal dust from spreading) for further use.

Picnic Barbecues

There are many models and ingenious designs to take your pick from. Some are rectangular in shape, others circular. Most picnic barbecues are simply scaled-down versions of their larger brethren, incorporating similar features such as windshields and adjustable grills. Some of the larger models have lids which, whilst providing shelter to food that is being grilled on a windy day, is very limiting when it comes to roasting and baking food by 'Indirect heat' (see page 14). Picnic barbecues that come supplied with fold-down or clip-in legs are far more comfortable to work with, and therefore a little safer than those 'legless' models that have to be set down on the ground.

Hibachis

In days past, the word 'hibachi' epitomised the art of barbecuing (the word, of Japanese origin, means fire-box, fire-bowl or, simply, brazier). Sizes can vary from a mere 10–12cm (4–5 inches) to a circular version around 41cm (16 inches) in diameter. Hibachis were originally made from cast metal but nowadays they are also available in pressed steel.

Beach Barbecues

It's quite fun to make an improvised beach barbecue. First scoop out a well a few inches deep – this will act as the barbecue's fire-bowl. Open up a channel into the well from the side hit by the prevailing wind so that a flow of air can get to the base of the fire. Then place a ring of large, dry stones around the edge of the well to act as a windbreak and support for the grill. Make sure there are gaps between the stones to allow the breeze to get through to the fire-bed. Collect dry driftwood for the fire, and once it is lit allow the wood to burn down to a bed of hot embers before cooking. Then use a piece of chicken wire as a temporary grill. The wire should be doubled over to reduce the size of the holes and provide extra rigidity. It is advisable to burn off the galvanised coating on the chicken wire prior to placing the food on it.

'Stay-at-home' units

Chiminerias

These units, sometimes referred to as 'Mexican barbecues', have a distinctive flask-like shape that makes the chimineria a very acceptable piece of garden sculpture (it could ultimately be transplanted into the garden landscape, perhaps with ivy climbing up through its chimney). With the chimineria's ability to burn both charcoal and wood one can, after the completion of an evening cookout, start placing logs on the fire, thus transforming the barbecue into a cosy patio heater. Chiminerias are available in cast aluminium, cast iron and handmade cast clay. In the last case, prior to purchase check that it is guaranteed to be frostproof. The fire-grate and cooking grill are usually made from cast iron. These ultra-heavyweight units should be sited on a firm level ground or base, but not directly onto wooden decking without there being adequate protection against scorching.

Brazier Barbecues

These are open-top units and can be either rectangular or circular, with or without wheels, and made from sheet or cast metal. Braziers invariably incorporate a windshield specifically designed to support a rotisserie. Some models incorporate a grill that rotates freely on an axis, but with most models it has to be adjusted by moving it into variable height slots on the face of the windshield.

Flat-top Barbecues

Flat-top units now occupy a very significant and fast-growing segment of the open-top category. Unlike the braziers, some of which can be fairly easily dismantled and transported, flat tops spend the whole of their working lives at their home base. With their cast-iron grills and griddle plates set in a sturdy hardwood trolley, these heavyweight units are strikingly similar in looks to gas-burning models (see page 168). They incorporate full-width easily removable ash pans, adjustable charcoal baskets (for heat control) and large wheels and casters for ease of manoeuvre.

Covered Barbecues

For those cooks with culinary aspirations far beyond the limitations inherent in an open barbecue, a barbecue with a vented lid is required. Barbecues that have a lid can be used, with great success, to roast and bake a wide and interesting variety of food. However, for many people, the main advantage that a covered barbecue has over an open unit is that it can be used for smoke-cooking meat and fish (see page 16). One of the most popular covered barbecues around is the kettle. The spherical-shaped version of the kettle has a grill and grate that sit in a permanently fixed position. The grill on the square-shaped kettle can, however, be adjusted to various heights and, very usefully, different inclinations. Some square kettle models also incorporate a rotisserie.

Smokers

Highly popular in the USA, the smoker is a multi-purpose barbecue that resembles an oversized cigar tube. The majority of smokers have two cooking grills sited one above the other, in the top half of the body. Most have a cylindrical body about 45cm (18 inches) in diameter and 100cm (40 inches) high, that provides sufficient space to handle up to 22kg (50 lb) of meat. This would allow you, for example, to smoke a ham on one of the grills and a turkey on the other. Situated in the base is a pan to hold the charcoal. Directly above that is the water pan. A small door on the side allows easy refuelling. Although the smoker can be used as a traditional grilling and roasting unit, it really comes into its own when cooking meat in a haze of moist steam generated by waves of moderate heat striking the water pan. See page 16 for details of the water smoker cooking technique.

Checklist for choosing a charcoal-burning barbecue

1. Check the stability of the barbecue, bearing in mind it will need to support a fully laden grill, plus a charcoal fire-bed. Give the unit a nudge to see whether it wobbles unduly.
   N.B. A wobble could well be due to a display unit's poor assembly, so do take that into account.
2. If the barbecue has a chrome-plated grill, check that it has no thin or bare patches.
3. If the barbecue has an adjustable-height grill that is supported by the windshield (the deeper the windshield the better), check that the grill slots easily into the shield, again bearing in mind that the grill will, at some stage, be fully laden and heavy to handle.
4. If buying a covered barbecue, check that its lid fits neatly and is not distorted. Ensure that the lid's air vent(s) can be easily adjusted.
5. If the barbecue has a mechanism for raising and lowering the grill, check that it operates smoothly.
6. Are the grill bars spaced closely enough to stop food, such as small sausages and chicken wings, falling through?
7. Make sure that there are no sharp edges to the barbecue's lid, fire-box or ash pan.

Wagons

These are the largest units in the covered barbecue category. The bigger wagon barbecues can comfortably cope with the flat food (burgers, steaks, etc.) demands of large parties and/or large joints of meat. Certain ultra-heavyweight wood-burning models, easily recognised by their distinctive smoke-stacks and large 'wagon wheels', are capable of handling and smoke-cooking very large quantities of food. These barbecues, known as pit barbecues in the USA, are now available in Europe. Most models have a heat indicator mounted in their lids. These gadgets are very useful in that they make baking and roasting a more precise exercise than would be the case if carried out in a covered barbecue minus a heat indicator. Virtually all wagons incorporate a warming rack, an exceedingly useful item. Retractable racks, i.e. those that swing back with the lid, when it is opened, are for me far more user-friendly than racks set in a permanently fixed position.

Guide to equipment

Built-in Charcoal Barbecues

These are readily available in DIY kit form. The basic kit usually comprises a chrome-plated grill, fire-grate, ash/fat tray and support brackets. Kits are supplied with detailed instructions on how to build a rectangular supporting brick structure, usually requiring around 100 bricks to complete. Tips on the design and location of an outdoor barbecue cooking area are set out on pages 178–80.

Gas barbecues

Gas barbecues enjoy several advantages over their charcoal-burning brethren whilst, at the same time, producing food that tastes, looks and smells just the same as that created by charcoal barbecues. Bear in mind that the barbecue taste is in fact created by the food itself – as the radiant heat (from whatever source) strikes it, the savoury juices released by the food vapourise and the resultant smoke haze rises up to embrace the food, to impart the distinctive taste, appearance and aroma so beloved by barbecue aficionados all over the world.

Most gas barbecues utilise a single layer of long-lasting volcanic rock, or ceramic briquettes, as their heat bed. There are, however, models where the traditional rock/briquettes heat bed has been supplanted by vitreous enamelled steel sections, cast-metal hearths or, in the case of a unique kettle design, a large vitreous enamelled steel cone.

Gas barbecues can be used with either butane or propane gas, but because the operating pressures for the two different types of gas are different, it is very important to use the correct regulator. Suffice to say, it is not possible to change from one gas to the other without also having to change the regulator.

The benefits of gas barbecues

1. They are easy to get going, even in windy conditions, in that most have push-button or rotary Piezo spark ignition. Conversely, after cooking has been completed, they are just as readily turned off. This latter asset is, in my personal opinion, of particular importance when considering the

unnecessary waste of energy that usually occurs when a charcoal fire-bed is left alone, after cooking, to extinguish itself an hour or so later.

2. They are ready for use only 5–10 minutes after ignition. This helps enormously in that it leaves the cook/host in a more relaxed state of mind when having to juggle fire-lighting, and getting the food and drink together in the hectic run-up to the party.

3. They are very economical. This can create a potential problem in that a cylinder of gas appears to be everlasting, particularly if the barbecue is being utilised on relatively few occasions through-out the year. Sod's law dictates that the gas will run out soon after you start cooking. So beware!

4. Cooking heat is easily and precisely controlled by adjusting a knob (rather than by raising and lowering the food, or opening and closing air vents).

5. They are, to a fair degree, self-cleaning (see page 177).

Portable

Like their charcoal counterparts, portable gas barbe-cues are eminently suited for holiday use, but even more so due to the added bonus that they can be pressed into service at the drop of a hat for general cooking duties. Models vary considerably in weight, power, design and cooking capacity. The lightweight units are, in general, powered by universally available disposable gas cartridges. The smallest cartridges provide approximately 1 1/2 hours of cooking time. Most portable units can be hooked up to standard gas cylinders which are greatly more economical to use.

'Stay-at-home' units

Gas barbecues in this category, due to their greater bulk and weight, will normally remain tied to their owner's abode.

Flat-top Gas Barbecues

These units are rapidly increasing in popularity amongst the world's barbecuers. At first glance they appear very similar to their charcoal-burning cousins, but of course display two, three or four burner control knobs. Like the charcoal units, they also feature cooking surfaces split between a cast metal grill and cast metal griddle (usually a 50–50 or $^1/_3$–$^2/_3$ split). The multi-burner format, coupled with multi-purpose cooking surfaces, makes this type of gas barbecue a highly versatile unit. A pull-out, full-width, drip tray, positioned in the base of the barbecue, ensures that the patio surface etc. is kept grease-free. A flat, full-size lid is provided to protect the cooking surfaces and burners from bad weather, and the attention of marauding cats.

N.B. Some flat tops can be converted to a wagon (covered) barbecue by fitting a roasting hood.

Wagon Gas Barbecues

Like the charcoal-burning models referred to on page 167, these come in a wide range of sizes and cooking capacities. The smallest units have a cooking area of around 200sq cm (32sq inches) and the largest up to a massive 4000sq cm (640sq inches). Apart from the smaller models, most wagon gas barbecues have a heat indicator mounted in their lids and include a warming rack. Power ratings vary from 11,000 BTU (3 kilowatts) to 50,000 BTU (14.5 kilowatts).

Burners

Burners are to gas barbecues as engines are to cars. As with anything else, you usually get what you pay for, so be aware that there can be a big variation in terms of quality, performance and durability. Some wagon gas barbecues have, in addition to the main burners, a burner that is mounted adjacent to the hood. These very useful outside burners, usually referred to as side burners, allow the cook to prepare soups, vegetables, sauces and hot drinks whilst grilling, roasting or baking is taking place on the adjacent grill. For me, a side burner (the more powerful the better) makes the ideal location to mount a small wok and indulge in a bout of stir-frying, braising, deep-frying or steaming. Hints on how to use your gas barbecue for wok-cooking are given on page 19.

Another auxiliary burner that one occasionally comes across in the more expensive wagon units is the rotisserie burner. Located at the rear of the grill area, the heat radiating from the burner impacts the rotating meat from behind, thus allowing the fats and juices to fall freely and directly into a drip pan. A further advantage that these units have is that one can spit-roast with the hood of the barbecue in the shut position, which is a great deal more efficient, particularly during windy conditions, than is the case when spit-roasting with an open unit.

Built-in Gas Barbecues

For some barbecue enthusiasts the idea of installing a built-in gas barbecue in a garden landscape has considerable appeal. The concept first became popular in California during the 1950s, when many of the dwellings built during that period invariably incorporated an outdoor cooking and eating area in their overall design. Whilst the structure (usually brick or stone) within which the barbecue sits is certainly permanent, the barbecue itself is removable for winter storage, unless, that is, one is contemplating using the facility all year round. Gas barbecues that are suitable for this kind of use range from wagons (minus their undercarriage) to flat tops (minus their trolley).

Check-list for choosing a gas barbecue

1. Check that the barbecue has been CE-Approved (for the European market) or by the official approval authority in North America and other countries throughout the world. The barbecue should carry a sticker to that effect. If in doubt, check its safety and technical credentials with the retailer.
2. Are the burner controls conveniently situated?
3. Check the barbecue's stability. Can it be fairly easily manoeuvred?
   Warning: Never attempt to move a gas barbecue when its burners are alight.
4. Has sufficient volcanic rock or ceramic briquettes been provided? There should be enough to cover the fire-grate in a single crowded layer.
   N.B. A smallish gap around the perimeter of the grate is fine, but largish gaps could permit fats to descend directly onto the burners, which could result in a flare-up.

Guide to equipment

Tools and accessories

In keeping with the fun nature of barbecuing, some tools and accessories may appear to border on the frivolous. All of the items featured below can, however, be useful to the barbecue cook. Novice barbecue cooks should concentrate their attention on those tools that help to make barbecuing easier and safer, tongs, gloves and forks being the first tools to obtain. Other tools and accessories can be added later.

Apron and Gloves
For comfort and practicality, nothing beats a cotton apron. It should be long enough to cover one's knees and ideally have a couple of deep pockets in the front in which to stash a roll of kitchen paper, matches etc. From clammy experience, I can assure you that wearing a plastic-coated apron whilst standing over a hot barbecue, is tantamount to wearing an overcoat in a sauna! Buy gloves rather than mitts – and gauntlets rather than gloves, because wrists and the lower forearm need some protection too. The glove's design should allow tools to be gripped firmly and comfortably, and the fabric, coupled with heat-resistant padding, should give effective protection against the barbecue's considerable radiant heat.

Basting Brushes
Long-handled basting brushes are readily available but some barbecue cooks like to use a couple of good-quality 5cm (2 inch) paint brushes, one to apply the oils and the other for applying sauces. The brushes' bristles should be natural; nylon and other man-made fibres are unsuitable.

Bug Repellents
Bug repellents, in spray or citronella candle form, are worth having around for warm summer evenings. You might even wish to consider investing in an electronic 'bug zapper' (similar to those found in food establishments).

Chopping Boards
The larger the board, the better. Ideally it should be made from plastic or laminate but a good-quality hard-wood board will suffice, providing it is scrupulously cleaned immediately after every cookout.

Grill-cleaning Brushes
The problem with most grill-cleaning brushes is that after relatively little use their fine wire bristles invariably clog up with fat and food debris. This then leaves you with the messy task of cleaning the cleaning brush! A cheaper alternative by far, which I find quite satisfactory, is a foil ball (see 'Foil', opposite). The metal scraper blade, which most brushes incorporate, is very handy for scraping off burnt-on fatty deposits on the upper and lower housings of the barbecue and for doing likewise with a greasy griddle plate.

Drip Pans
Roasting meat by the 'Indirect heat' method (see page 14) is a cooking technique that all owners of covered barbecues will become very familiar with. For most covered units, this method of cooking calls for a drip pan to be placed immediately underneath the area of the grill where the meat or poultry is to be sited. A drip pan, so positioned, catches the falling fats and juices thus helping to keep the base of the barbecue in a cleaner state than otherwise would be the case. A standard steel roasting tin used as a drip pan will require cleaning out and washing at the completion of every cook-out. One can purchase lightweight drip pans made from aluminium, which can be discarded after just one outing, but for lazy, mean-minded cooks like me, making a drip pan from a roll of foil is profoundly more satisfying and rewarding. It not only saves money, but it allows me to skip the irksome cleaning task referred to above. Incidentally, it is much easier to remove the pan from the barbecue for 'binning' once its fatty contents have been allowed to partly congeal.

To make a drip pan from foil
Take a 46cm (18 inch) roll of heavy-duty foil and tear off a strip about 10cm (4 inches) longer than the length of the proposed pan. Fold the foil in half lengthways, double-fold the edges to make 2.5cm (1 inch) walls, flatten the foil walls and lightly score a bisecting line at each corner. Pull out and pinch the corners before folding them tightly back against the sides. The result should be a leak-proof pan approximately 13cm (5 inches) wide with walls 2.5cm (1 inch) high. To create a wider and larger pan, use wider foil or simply fold the foil widthways.

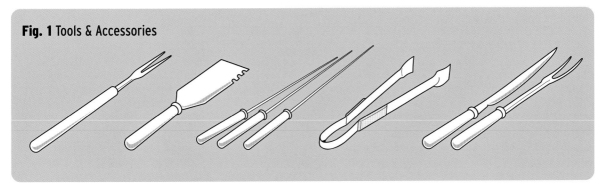

Fig. 1 Tools & Accessories

First Aid Kit
Suffering the small burn and blister is par for the course during a busy barbecue year. A spray-on burn lotion would therefore make a useful addition to your home first-aid kit.

Foil
Aluminium foil is indispensable to the barbecue cook. Try to purchase the 'heavy duty' foil rather than the more flimsy variety, especially if it is your intention to make your own drip pans (see opposite). Foil can also be used for making a temporary griddle plate and, when crumpled into a ball, for removing burnt-on food deposits from grill bars, spit rods and metal skewers.

Forks
Forks should be long-handled with a comfortable wooden or PVC grip.

Gas Lighters
Also known as gas matches, these products are particularly handy for owners of gas barbecues that do not incorporate a Piezo igniter. In fact they are well worth having around as a stand-by for those who own units that do have this excellent gizmo. Gas lighters are also very effective for getting solid firelighters going, lighting garden flares, etc.

Hinged Wire Holders
Chrome-plated hinged wire holders come in many different shapes and sizes. The square, rectangular or round ones are excellent for handling quantities of chicken wings, cocktail sausages, chicken livers and the like that are small enough to fall through the grill bars of some barbecues. It therefore follows that the bars of the holder should themselves be closely spaced. Holders used in this fashion are very handy in that one can turn over several pieces of food at one time and, providing the bars of the holder have been well oiled, it is far less likely that the food will stick to the barbecue's grill bars. Some holders have pockets shaped to accommodate up to half a dozen burgers or chops. These can also be pressed into service for toasting bread and burger buns. There are also the cylindrical or rectangular box-shaped holders which, when clamped to a spit rod, allow small pieces of food to tumble about freely as the spit rotates.

Fish Holders
Particularly useful are holders designed for fish, which can be particularly fragile to handle when they are partially cooked and need turning. The most common will accommodate a single fish, such as a trout, weighing up to around 375g (12oz), with the largest single fish holders able to hold a fish weighing in at around 1kg (2 lb). Another version that is available will hold three fish, each around 375g (12oz), side by side. Sardines are pernickety to handle, but there is a holder that looks something like a bicycle wheel, which can contain up to 12 of these little fish.

Kitchen Paper
Vital for mopping up spills, mopping brows, spreading oil over fish and grill bars, wrapping around hot sausages to protect guests' fingers and the wiping of children's runny noses!

Knives and Cutlery
A good-quality butcher's knife is required for trimming and portioning meat. A small paring knife will also be required for preparing fruit and vegetables, and a sharp carving knife is essential for tackling roasts. We all know that cutting through a less than tender steak or a carbon-coated sausage, whilst balancing a plastic

Guide to equipment

plate on one's lap, can be a daunting and inevitably messy task. In these circumstances anything less than really sharp steak knives will not do.

Meat Thermometers
A meat thermometer helps to take the guesswork out of cooking large joints, particularly useful when checking whether a joint of pork is fully cooked. Meat thermometers are generally available in two styles: those with a round, clock face with a moving hand that broadly tells you if the meat you are cooking is rare, medium or well done, and the arrow-shaped thermometer that has a column of mercury from which the meat's inner temperature can be read. With either type, a false reading will occur if the tip of the pointed probe touches bone or spit rod. Do not leave the thermometer in the meat during the cooking process as the glass may shatter, and the face of the thermometer will quickly become coated with burnt fat and thus prove very difficult to read.

Paint Scrapers
These are the professional's choice for removing food debris and fat from griddle plates. Buy a new one for culinary use only.

Pots and Pans
Pans should have long handles which, if wooden or plastic, can be wrapped in foil to protect them when directly over the barbecue's grill. The pans should have thick bases and, for the sake of domestic harmony, a pan or two, solely for barbecue use, should be purchased.

Skewers
Metal skewers with a flat, or twisted, blade are best for spearing chunky pieces of meat and/or vegetables. Round, small-diameter skewers tend to leave the food behind when turned. The best skewers for holding food firmly in position are the twin-pronged versions. Bamboo skewers, traditionally used for satay and small appetisers, should be well soaked in water before use to prevent them burning up before the food is fully cooked.

Rotisseries
Whilst relatively few barbecues come supplied with a rotisserie (also known as a spit-roast assembly) as standard, most barbecue manufacturers do include a rotisserie set in their range of accessories. Virtually all charcoal brazier models have windshields that will accommodate a rotisserie. The bottom casing of all wagon gas barbecues is designed to do likewise. The vast bulk of spit motors are battery operated, and the most efficient of which work off two HP2 batteries. The plastic housing of the single-battery motor is very vulnerable to the effects of the heat emitted from the barbecue. Wrapping two or three layers of foil around the casing beforehand will help to prevent 'meltdown'. Badly balanced food on the spit rod will result in the motor undergoing excessive wear. Apart from carrying out the spit-balance test (see page 18) the best solution is to use a set of balance weights. Using an adjustable weight when spit-roasting an irregular shaped joint, such as a leg of lamb, will ensure a smooth rotation and thereby help to reduce wear and tear on the motor. You may, however, have a little trouble in tracking a set of weights down.

Spatulas
Spatulas should be long-handled, with a broad slotted blade to allow some of the food's fat to drain through. The scissor-action of twin-bladed spatulas allows the cook to grip and position the food more easily than the single-bladed version.

Tongs
A good pair of tongs is, without any shadow of doubt, the single most important tool in the cook's arsenal. It is well worth taking the trouble to seek out a pair that not only suits your strength of hand but will allow you to manoeuvre, and cleanly pick up a chipolata without catapulting the food at some innocent bystander! A good, pre-purchase test is to use the tongs to pick up a pencil. The 'mouth' should grip the food gently but firmly – sharp teeth may pierce the sealed surface of the food and allow some of the precious juices to escape.

Woks
A wok and a gas barbecue constitute the ideal cooking partnership. There is more about the wok and wok-cooking on page 19. When purchasing your wok, try to find one that includes a set of wok tools, i.e. a ladle and a shovel.

Safety precautions

Gas barbecues ... some do's & don'ts

After assembling your new barbecue, your first task before commencing to use it, is to spend time reading and inwardly digesting the notes in the manufacturer's operating manual, on safety and how to get the best use from your unit. Safety really should be first, and christening your new barbecue should come second!

- Do carry out a leak test before fitting the hose, valve and regulator. All of these are normally supplied interconnected, although, with some models, you may be required to supply and fit the regulator to the barbecue's control panel.

  To carry out the test:
  1. Make up a soap and water solution.
  2. Take your full gas cylinder and the hose, valve and regulator assembly to an outside area and connect the regulator to the cylinder valve.
  3. Turn the control knob(s) of the barbecue valve(s) to the 'off' position.
  4. Turn the gas supply on at the cylinder.
  5. Apply the soapy mixture to all the connection points, from, and including, the cylinder. valve to the valve(s) at the end of the hose.
  6. Check each connection point for bubbles caused by leaks. Tighten any leaking connections (any item that leaks persistently must be replaced).
  7. Turn off the gas supply at the cylinder and turn the control knob(s) to the 'high' position to release the pressure in the hose. Disconnect the regulator from the cylinder and fit the assembly to the barbecue following the manufacturer's instructions.

- Do make sure you have a means of lighting the gas before turning on the supply.
- Do fully close the cylinder valve when the barbecue is not being used.
- Do store the cylinder outdoors in a well-ventilated place.
- Do keep the cylinder upright at all times.
- Do ensure that the lid of the barbecue is open before lighting the gas burners.
- Do allow at least 75cm (30 inches) of space between the barbecue and any flammable material (wood, etc).
- Do keep children and pets well away from all hot barbecues.
- Don't store the cylinder of gas in direct sunlight.
- Don't smoke or use a naked flame when testing for gas leaks.
- Don't store or use petrol, or any other volatile liquids or vapours, near the barbecue.
- Don't adjust your gas barbecue indoors or in any confined, unventilated area.
- Don't move a gas barbecue when it is lit.

Preparing the charcoal fire-bed

For grilling, wok-cooking or griddle plate cooking

First build a pyramid-shaped pile of charcoal in the centre of the fire-grate.

If using solid firelighters, insert two or three pieces well into the lower half of the pile. After lighting, the starter will burn for about 15 minutes depending on the type of barbecue and wind strength. When most of the coals are covered by a grey ash, spread them over the grate (if wok-cooking, leave the pyramid intact) one layer deep, and leave alone until the coals are completely covered in ash. You can now start to cook.

Tip: During the early stages of fire-lighting, particularly if the wind is up, keep an eye on the pieces of fire-lighter to make sure they are burning well and have not gone out.

If using liquid firelighter, follow the manufacturer's instructions carefully. Take care not to use too much liquid, particularly with barbecues that incorporate air vents in their fire-bowl as excess liquid may drain out of the barbecue and accidentally ignite.

If using jellied alcohol, squeeze small amounts of jelly into cavities near the base of the charcoal pyramid. Close and remove the tube, and light the jelly as soon as possible.

Guide to equipment

If using a gas torch, arrange the charcoal on the grate one layer deep and closely together. Light the gas and adjust the flame, and then play the flame slowly over the fuel until grey patches appear.

For spit-roasting

Position a pile of charcoal on the fire-grate towards the rear of the fire-bowl and light as described above. The spit-roast cooking technique is covered on page 19.

For roasting, smoke-cooking & baking by 'Indirect heat'

(N.B. Applicable only to covered barbecues, e.g. kettles)

Having ensured that the barbecue's lower vents are fully open, place a pan (an old roasting tin will suffice) in the centre of the fire-grate or, if your unit is a round 'kettle' model, clip its charcoal retention rails into position. Place two solid firelighters, about 10 cm (4 inches) apart, on each side of the grate. Having covered the firelighters with the required number of briquettes (for your first attempt at 'Indirect Heat' cooking, around 40 briquettes per side should prove adequate to tackle the Sunday roast), light them with a long match or taper. The time it will take for the fire to become established could vary from 30 minutes to 60 minutes depending on the number of firelighters used and wind strength, i.e. if you are in a hurry, double up the firelighters. The 'Indirect heat' cooking technique is covered on page 14.

Heat control

When the fire-bed has been prepared, and the fire is making steady progress, you are left free to concentrate your attention on cooking the food and controlling the heat.

Controlling the heat that emanates from a charcoal-burning barbecue is not as simple, or precise, as the instant control achieved with a gas barbecue. One can, however, adopt the following methods:

- by adjusting the lower air vents in a covered barbecue (the vent in the lid of a covered barbecue should always be left open during cooking);
- By altering the distance between fire-bed and grill by means of rotating grills, adjustable levers etc.
- By increasing or decreasing the distance between individual briquettes, or pieces of lumpwood charcoal, once they are alight: the closer the lumps of fuel, the more intense the resulting heat.
- Food is cooked by the infrared radiation given off by the hot coals, so anything that masks the radiation will slow down the cooking process. Periodically tapping off excess ash (rapping the rim of the barbecue's fire-bowl should do the trick) will produce a small surge in temperature – conversely, leaving the ashes in situ will help to dampen an over-hot fire.

Tip: If you are engaged in a protracted open-grill cooking session, keep a reserve of briquettes around, but not quite touching the live coals. Cold briquettes, when added directly to hot coals will, momentarily, dampen down the fire whereas pre-warmed briquettes, when nudged up against hot coals, will not produce such an adverse effect. The other benefit is that unused charcoal can be retrieved at the completion of the cookout for future use.

Flaming flare-ups!

Some barbecue cooks believe a flare-up (sudden blaze) is a cross that all who stand at the helm of a barbecue have to occasionally put up with. Some people are in fact convinced that a mighty flare-up is an essential element in the barbecue ritual due to their seeing photographs of food-laden barbecues with flames (usually phoney) leaping skyward. However, apart from those cooks who actually set out with intent to flame-cook, my advice is to avoid flare-ups like the plague! One of the problems with a flare-up is that it can, unless you react fast, quickly spoil the appearance of the food. Chicken portions, on their way to becoming 'cremated', get covered in a black, greasy film which requires wiping clean with kitchen paper before you carry on cooking.

The worst flare-ups are created by excessive heat striking excessively fatty food. Unless one reacts very smartly, the fat raining down onto the fire-bed will quickly boost the flames into a mini-inferno. It would, however, be virtually impossible to avoid creating a flare-up, even using a fairly moderate cooking heat, if the entire grill was completely covered with fatty food such as sausages, burgers, chicken portions or lamb cutlets, etc.

How to avoid flare-ups with charcoal units

Regardless of the quantity of food that has to be barbecued, refrain from covering all the grate with charcoal because, in the event of a flare-up, there would be no alternative but to remove all food from the grill. The answer is to use a pair of tongs and arrange the hot briquettes so that roughly one-third of the grate is covered with charcoal crowded closely together, and on another one-third the charcoal briquettes, or pieces of lumpwood, are set about 5cm (2 inches) apart. Leave the remaining area completely devoid of fuel. This suggestion could be particularly useful when you have to tackle a batch of steaks where each guest requires a different degree of doneness for their steak – you can quickly seal the surfaces of each steak over the 'hot spot' before moving it to the adjacent moderate heat sector. The fully cooked or partly cooked steaks can be parked up over the 'vacant lot'. With a little practice you should be able to rustle up steaks to order, with everyone tucking into their steak at the same time.

Another fat/flare-up-reducing exercise, when confronted with the prospect of barbecuing a large quantity of chicken pieces or large sausages, is to place them in a roasting tin, cover loosely with foil and gently sweat in a moderate oven or in a covered barbecue (using Indirect heat) for about 30 minutes or so. In losing a good deal of their fat they will take on a somewhat lacklustre appearance, but will regain their good looks during subsequent grilling. Try to time this so that it takes place as close to the cookout as possible, and remember to keep the part-cooked food covered and in a cool place.

Tip: By tilting the barbecue slightly towards the 'vacant lot', with grill bars facing in the same direction, some of the fat and juices from the food will trickle down the bars to drop off into a pre-positioned drip pan.

Tip: Before grilling spare ribs or pork cutlets, seal them, with 2–3 tablespoons water, in a foil package and heat in a moderate oven (or in a covered barbecue) for about 40 minutes. This will render out a lot of the fat, thus considerably reducing the possibility of a flare-up and greatly shortening the cooking time.

Snuffing out the fire

One of charcoal's great attributes is that it will, once lit, carry on burning steadily until it has been reduced to a grey ash. This however, is particularly wasteful, in every sense of the word, if there is a goodly amount of solid charcoal left when cooking has been completed. With covered barbecues, the fire can be snuffed out by closing the top and bottom dampers. The hot charcoal should be extinguished in about 30 minutes. With open models, the charcoal can either be carefully transferred to a lidded metal coal bucket, or dumped into a pail of water for later draining and drying. Never pour water over hot charcoal in the barbecue. Doing so could badly damage the unit.

Gas barbecues 'troubleshooter'

BURNERS WILL NOT LIGHT

Possible cause: The cylinder of gas is almost empty.
Solution: Replace with a full cylinder.

Possible cause: The cylinder valve is not fully open.
Solution: Fully open the cylinder valve (turn the valve anti-clockwise).

Possible cause: The valve outlets are not properly seated in the venturi.
Solution: Fully locate the valve in the venturi (when properly in position, the gas jets are visible through the 'window' in the venturi).

Possible cause: One or more of the gas jets or venturis is clogged (perhaps with spider webs or cocoons – quite possible if the barbecue has not been used for some time).
Solution: Clean the inside of the venturi tubes with a bottle brush. Carefully clean the jet orifices with fine wire or the tip of a round toothpick – do not enlarge the hole.

Guide to equipment

Possible cause: The venturis are not properly seated.
Solution: Check that the retaining spring, if used, is properly engaged.

Possible cause: A sharp kink in the flexible gas hose.
Solution: Re-position the cylinder to straighten the hose.

Possible cause: The igniter is not working.
Solution:
a) Check the assembly instruction to ascertain if the gap between the electrode cover is correct (if it is correct, a spark should be visible);
b) Ensure that all wires are intact and connected;
c) Check the ceramic component for cracks (if a new igniter assembly is required, use a long taper in the meantime).

Possible cause: A defective valve or regulator.
Solution: If you suspect either of the above items are faulty, remove the hose from the barbecue and take it, along with the regulator and cylinder, to an authorised servicing bottle gas dealer for inspection.

BURNERS PROVIDE INSUFFICIENT HEAT

Possible cause: The barbecue is not given sufficient time to warm up.
Solution: Increase the warm-up time by several minutes to allow for low air temperatures and strong breezes.

Possible cause: The venturis and gas jets are not properly aligned.
Solution: Fully locate the valve in the venturi.

Possible cause: Some of the vents in the burner assembly are clogged with food debris.
Solution: Brush clean (using a brass or stainless steel bristle brush).

Possible cause: An excessive amount of volcanic rock is used.
Solution: Remove sufficient rock to allow a close-packed single layer only.

Possible cause: One, or more, of the gas jets or venturis is clogged.
Solution: Clean the inside of the venturi with a bottle brush. Carefully clean the jet orifices with fine wire or the tip of a round toothpick.

Possible cause: The volcanic rock is heavily permeated with food debris and fat
Solution:
a) Wash the rocks in hot water to which a biological soap (powder or tablet) solution has been added. Change the water and repeat as necessary. Make sure the volcanic rock is thoroughly dry before using it for cooking. Dry it either in the barbecue with the lid down or in the kitchen oven;
b) Alternatively, burn the rocks clean – see 'Care and cleaning', opposite.

FLASHBACK (FLAME IN OR AROUND THE VENTURI)
If flashback should occur, immediately shut off the barbecue burner-controls and then the cylinder valve off.

Possible cause: The venturis have become blocked when the barbecue has cooled.
Solution: Clean the inside of the tube with a bottle brush.

Possible cause: The venturis are not properly seated.
Solution: Check that the retaining spring (if used) is present and engaged.

Possible cause: The valve outlets are not properly seated in the venturi.
Solution: Fully locate the valve in the venturi.

Possible cause: The vents in the burner assembly are clogged.
Solution: Brush clean, using a brass or stainless-steel bristle brush. (If a wire brush is unavailable, clear the blocked vents with a piece of fine wire or a round toothpick.)

Possible cause: The barbecue is exposed to strong winds.
Solution: Shield the middle/lower half of the barbecue from the wind (or turn off the gas and move the barbecue to a more sheltered position).

BURNER FLAME IS EXCESSIVELY YELLOW

Possible cause: The burner holes are clogged.
Solution: Brush clean with a brass or stainless steel bristle brush.

Possible cause: The venturis tubes are blocked.
Solution: Clean the inside of the venturi tube with a bottle brush.

Possible cause: The venturis are not properly located on the valve outlets.
Solution: Check that the retaining spring, if used, is properly engaged.

Care & cleaning

All barbecues tend to become somewhat gungy after only a few cookouts. Hygienic considerations aside, allowing your barbecue to get progressively dirtier makes it less efficient. It therefore pays to get into the habit of giving the grill(s) and, if the unit has one, the griddle plate, a basic clean after every cooking session. There are a variety of ways to tackle the job. Some people have adopted the 'wet newspaper' method. This involves spreading several sheets of newspaper on the ground, and giving them a good soaking before laying the grill(s) (which should preferably still be warm) on top. A few more sheets of paper are placed over the grill(s) and these are also soaked. The theory has it that when the grill(s) is removed some hours later the encrusted fat and food debris will be left behind (some might say appropriately) with the newsprint. Using a wire brush is the preferred cleaning method, but brushes with fine wire bristles can quickly become clogged.

My personal preference is simplicity itself: loosely crumple up a good-size piece of foil and, with gloved hand, press the ball of foil firmly down onto the warm grill bars, scrubbing along the line of bars to remove all the food encrustations. A quick wipe with some kitchen paper and the barbecue is ready for its next outing. During the next warm-up you can if you wish give the bars a further wipe-over with kitchen paper, but in the meantime the heat will have acted as an effective cauterant. If you have a large sink (a shallow seed tray or something similar will do) giving the grill an occasional soak in hot water, in which biological soap (powder or tablet) has been dissolved, should produce sparkling results.

Gas barbecues

Giving the grills and fire-bed (volcanic rock or ceramic briquettes) on your covered gas barbecue a basic clean after every cookout is easy and straightforward: having removed all the food from the grill, and with the barbecue still alight, close the lid and adjust all the burner controls to the high setting. Leave the barbecue for 5–10 minutes, which should be long enough for most, if not all, the fat and food residues to burn off the grills and some of the fats to burn out of the rocks. Be warned, however, that during the first few minutes of 'burn off' a considerable volume of smoke could issue from under the lid, so make sure doors and windows are closed or well upwind of the barbecue.

The alternative method, carried out just prior to lighting up, is to turn over all the cold rocks or briquettes and add an extra minute or two to the warm-up period. A perfect way to kill two birds with one stone!

Annual spring clean

This does not necessarily have to be undertaken in springtime, but giving your gas barbecue a thorough cleaning once or twice a year (twice if you are an 'all-year-rounder') will help to keep your unit in tip-top working order. Proceed as follows:

1. Remove the grill(s), volcanic rocks or briquettes, burner and igniter assemblies.
2. Cover the valve outlets with foil.
3. Scrape and wire-brush the inside surfaces of the barbecue's upper and lower housings to remove food debris. Clean off the surface with hot water and mild detergent using a scrubbing brush or scouring pad.
4. Brush the surfaces of the burners with a wire brush. Clean out any clogged vents with a piece of stiff wire.

5. Remove the foil from the valve outlets, clean the jet orifices (using fine wire) and replace the burner (ensuring the valve outlets are inside the venturi), and igniter assemblies. Replace the fire-grate and rocks or briquettes.
6. If the barbecue has a window in its lid, clean the glass (when it is cold) using hot water and a mild cleanser. Do not use a commercial oven cleaner.
7. Clean and treat any wood shelving and support structure with an approved wood preservative.
8. Clean the grill(s) as described on page 177.
9. Clean out the drip pan or drip tray.
10. Finally tighten up all nuts and bolts in the frame assembly.

Tricks of the trade

Taking your gas barbecue's 'heat fingerprints'

Burner configurations on gas barbecues vary quite considerably from manufacturer to manufacturer. Small portable units and the smallest wagon models have a single rectangular burner, usually referred to as a 'ribbon burner', positioned in the centre of the lower casing. The shape of burners in wagon gas barbecues can vary from a squared figure of eight to an H-shape. Flat-top gas barbecues invariably have multiple, evenly spaced, narrow ribbon burners made from cast metal. The shape, size and location of the barbecue's burners (in relation to the cooking area they are serving), together with their power output, greatly influences the manner and speed in which the food is cooked.

Experience will eventually make you aware of where the hot, medium and cool spots on your barbecue grill are, but an easy and tasty way to ascertain the heat distribution pattern of your new gas barbecue (its 'fingerprints') is to conduct Uncle Jim's Toast Test.

Uncle Jim's Toast Test
For this you will require a loaf of sliced white bread. Try to choose a calm day, or a sheltered spot, to conduct the test – preferably around tea time.

1. Light the burners in the usual manner. If your unit is one of the covered models, close the lid.

2. Leave the barbecue to warm up for about ten minutes.
3. Adjust the control knob(s) to the medium heat setting and leave for a further 2–3 minutes.
4. Having opened the lid, should there be one, completely cover the surface of the grill(s) with slices of the bread and leave for about two minutes or until the underside of the bread is nicely browned.
5. Using tongs, turn each slice of bread in situ to reveal, by the gradation of the slices' colour, where the grill's hottest and coolest areas are.

In order to gain maximum kudos from the above highly scientific test, I suggest that you finish off toasting the bread and lavishly anoint the crisp golden slices with butter and strawberry jam, before dishing out the 'naughty but nice' slices to a highly appreciative family. It's a great way to start building up your alfresco culinary reputation!

A few tips on constructing an outdoor barbecue cooking area

An ideal time to sit down quietly and plan a barbecue area is when your new garden landscape is being prepared, or an existing garden layout is being altered. Should the former be the case and if it happens to coincide with the construction of a new dwelling, so much the better, as this will provide you with the satisfying opportunity to match bricks and materials for the barbecue's support structure.

Using organic stone for the structural framework has its drawbacks in that it can prove somewhat difficult for the amateur bricklayer to work with. In addition, natural stone can appear somewhat incongruous when standing alongside brick. The same comment could also apply to a structure made from red housing bricks set against the back-drop of warm, honey-coloured stone walls. Many people, quite wisely, opt for reconstituted stone blocks which are readily available, reasonably cheap to buy and fairly simple for the handyman

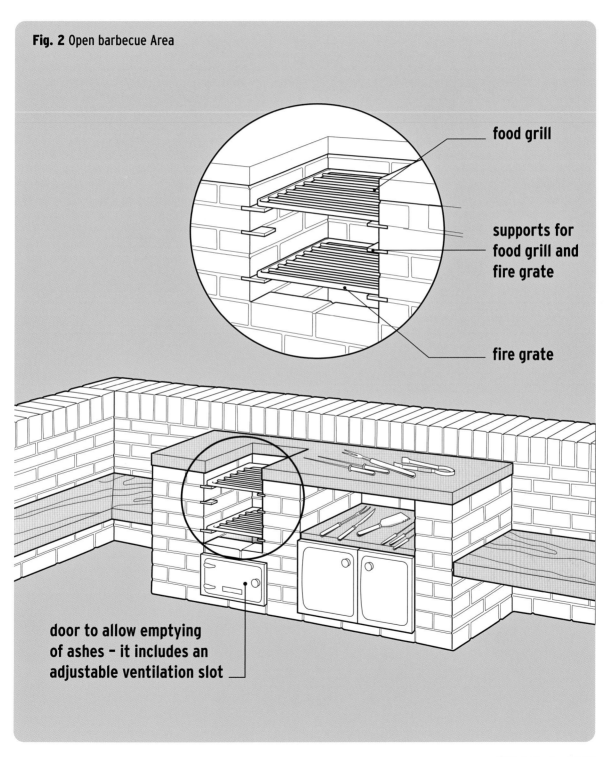

Fig. 2 Open barbecue Area

food grill

supports for
food grill and
fire grate

fire grate

door to allow emptying
of ashes - it includes an
adjustable ventilation slot

Guide to equipment

to work with. Considerable care should be taken over the barbecue's design, layout and location, because errors at this stage may not be easy to rectify at a later date, particularly if this involves digging up concrete foundations and knocking down a solid brick or stone edifice!

Careful consideration should also be given to the work surface immediately adjacent to the barbecue itself. Ideally, it should be of a size adequate to comfortably accommodate chopping boards, tools, condiments and serving dishes. For those going the whole hog, there could also be a separate work surface for use by the commis (deputy) chef to prepare salads etc. Cupboards set underneath the work surface, while not essential, again would be useful for storing fuel or, out of season, gardening equipment.

Should it be your intention to hold 'evening into night-time' barbecue parties it makes good sense to grab the opportunity, at the pre-construction stage, to have a power cable laid to the barbecue area. This, however, is a job for a competent electrician to tackle – it is better to be safe and sure. Having had the power cable installed, you will then be able to mount at least one spotlight covering the general area around the barbecue, particularly important if there are hazards present in the shape of steps, ponds, prickly bushes, bird baths, statues, etc. Equally, if not more, important is having a spotlight positioned directly above the barbecue to enable the cook to at least discern whether the food on the grill is in a burnt or unburnt state. If there is to be only one light source, avoid positioning it directly behind the cook as doing so will only make matters worse by the creation of a deep shadow over the barbecue's cooking surface.

For the sake of good hygiene, there should be two buckets of hot water, plus a bar of soap, nail brush and towels, handily placed for the cook and his or her helpers to use. The water should be regularly renewed during the cookout. However, where expense is no object, a small sink with running water (bliss for blistered fingers), adjacent to the work surface, would be a very useful luxury.

If there is adequate space, insert four small concrete bases in the ground around the perimeter of the barbecue area, on which to mount the legs of a garden canopy. Apart from keeping the cook, food, and helpers dry in wet weather (coping with a batch of burgers with one hand, whilst the other hand is grasping an umbrella, is not an easy task), a canopy will also shelter cook and helpers from the sun's rays.

If the built-in barbecue has to be located fairly close to the house, try to ascertain, prior to commencing work, how the wind generally behaves in that particular spot, bearing in mind that if windows or French doors are accidentally left open during cooking they could act as a conduit for aroma-rich smoke to permeate throughout the house. This could well result in your furniture, furnishings and resident pets, taking on a smoky barbecue flavour!

Turf will quickly become worn and increasingly slippery, particularly in the early evening, when subjected to heavy foot traffic. So for safety's sake, the area immediately surrounding the cooking and serving points should be either paved with non-slip concrete slabs or covered with a roughened concrete or gravel surface. Finally, do site the barbecue well away from trees and shrubs – in fact any flammable material.

Cooking Times

ROASTING (USING 'INDIRECT HEAT')

Food	Cut	Degree of Cooking	Heat Setting	Internal Temperature	Approximate Minutes per 500g (I lb)
Beef	rib roast	rare	low/medium	60°C/140°F	18-20
		medium	low/medium	70°C/160°F	20-25
		well done	low/medium	77°C/170°F	25-30
	sirloin		medium	60-77°C/140-170°F	25-30
	rump/rolled		medium	65-77°C/150-170°F	25-30
Lamb	leg	rare	medium	60°C/140°F	18-22
		medium	medium	70°C/160°F	22-28
		well done	medium	77°C/170°F	28-33
	crown roast	rare	medium	60°C/140°F	25-30
		medium	medium	70°C/160°F	30-36
		well done	medium	77°C/170°F	36-42
	shoulder	medium	medium	70°C/160°F	22-28
		well done	medium	77°C/170°F	28-33
Pork	loin	well done	low/medium	85°C/185°F	25-30
	fresh ham	well done	low/medium	85°C/185°F	20-25
	crown	well done	low/medium	85°C/185°F	25-35
Veal	loin	well done	low/medium	85°C/185°F	20-25
	leg	well done	low/medium	85°C/185°F	20-25
	shoulder	well done	low/medium	85°C/185°F	20-25
Poultry	chicken	well done	low/medium	85°C/185°F	15-20
	turkey	well done	low/medium	85°C/185°F	12-20*
	duckling	well done	low/medium	85°C/185°F	15-20

*Cooking times will vary considerably according to the weight of the bird, i.e. the larger and heavier the bird, the faster the cooking time.

GRILLING Approximate cooking time (each side) in minutes

Food	Cut or Weight	Size	Heat Setting	Rare	Medium	Well Done
Beef	steak	2.5cm (1 inch)	high	3-4	4-5	5-6
	steak	4cm (1 ½ inches)	high	5-6	7-8	9-10
	steak*	5cm (2 inches)	high	7-8	9-10	10-11
	flank steak	whole	high	3-4+		
	hamburger	2.5cm (1 inch)	medium/high	3-4	5-6	6-8
Lamb	chops	2.5cm (1 inch)	medium/high	5-6	7-8	9-10
	liver**	1cm (1/2 inch)	medium/high		5-6	
Pork	chops	2.5cm (1 inch)	medium/high			15-18
	spare ribs	whole or section	medium			55-75
	liver**	1cm (½ inch)	medium/high		6-7	
	ham	2.5cm (1 inch)	medium			15-20
Poultry	chicken	1.5kg (3 ½ lb) (split)	medium			35-45
	duck	1.75kg (4 lb) (split)	medium	5-6	10-12	25-28
Veal	steak or chops	2.5cm (1 inch)	medium			9-12
Fish	steak	1cm (½ inch)	medium			2-3
	steak	2.5cm (1 inch)	medium			5
	whole fish: allow 10 minutes per 2.5cm (1 inch) of thickness					
	e.g. a fish 5cm (2 inches) thick will require 20 minutes cooking (10 minutes per side).					
	lobster	500-750 g (1-1 ½ lb)	medium/high			7-10

* If the steak is 5cm (2 inches) or more thick you can use a meat thermometer to judge - steak is rare at 55°C/130°F, well done at 77°C/170°F.

+ Maximum cooking time for the steak to remain tender.

** Avoid overcooking or the liver will become tough.

SPIT-ROASTING Approximate cooking time in hours*

Food	Cut or Weight	Size	Heat Setting	Rare 60°C/140°F	Medium 70°C/160°F	Well Done 77°C/170°F
Beef	rump	1.25-2.25kg (3-5 lb)	medium	1 1/2-2	2 1/4-3	3-4
	sirloin	2.25-2.75kg (5-6 lb)	medium/high	1 1/4-1 3/4	2 1/4-3	3-4
	rolled rib	1.75-2.75kg (4-6 lb)	medium/high	2-2 1/2	2 1/4-3	3 1/4-4
Lamb	leg	1.5-3.5kg (3 1/2-8 lb)	medium	1-1 1/4	1 1/2-2	2-3 1/4
	rolled shoulder	1.25-2.75kg (3-6 lb)	medium	1-1 1/4	1 1/2-2	2-3 1/4

Food	Cut or Weight	Size	Heat Setting			85°C/185°F
Pork	shoulder	1.25-2.75kg (3-6 lb)	medium/high			2-3
	loin	1.25-2.25kg (3-5 lb)	medium/high			2-3
	spare ribs	1-1.75kg (2-4 lb)	medium/high			1-1 3/4
	fresh ham	2.25-3.5kg (5-8 lb)	medium			3 1/2-4 1/2
Poultry	chicken	1.1-2.25kg (2 1/2-5 lb)	medium			1-1 1/2
	turkey	3.5-7kg (8-16 lb)	medium			2-4
	duckling	1.75-2.75kg (4-6 lb)	medium			1-2
Veal	leg	2.25-3.5kg (5-8 lb)	medium			2-3
	rolled shoulder	1.25-2.25kg (3-5 lb)	medium			1 1/2-2 1/2
	loin	2.25-2.75kg (5-6 lb)	medium			1 1/2-2 1/4

Food	Cut or Weight	Size	Heat Setting			50-55°C/120-130°F
Fish	large, whole	2.25-4.5kg (5-10 lb)	low/medium			1-1 1/4
	small, whole	750g-1.75kg (1 1/2-4 lb)	low/medium			1/2-1

* For accuracy, use a meat thermometer and cook to the internal temperatures given in the chart on page 181.

Conversion Charts

American and Australian Conversion Chart

Apart from the usual basic measures, such as 'teaspoon', 'tablespoon' and 'pinch', all the quantities and measurements in this book are given in both metric and imperial form. All spoon measures are level unless otherwise stated.

	BRITISH	AMERICAN	AUSTRALIAN
Teaspoons and tablespoons	1 teaspoon (5ml)	1 teaspoon (5ml)	1 teaspoon (5ml)
	1 tablespoon*	1 rounded tablespoon	1 scant tablespoon
	2 tablespoons	2 tablespoons	1$^1/_2$ tablespoons
	3 tablespoons	3 tablespoons	2$^1/_2$ tablespoons
	4 tablespoons	4 tablespoons	3$^1/_2$ tablespoons
	5 tablespoons	5 tablespoons	4$^1/_2$ tablespoons
Cup+ measures (liquid)	4 tablespoons	$^1/_4$ cup	$^1/_4$ cup
	125ml (4fl oz)	$^1/_2$ cup	$^1/_2$ cup
	250ml (8fl oz)	1 cup	1 cup
	450ml ($^3/_4$ pint)	2 cups	2 cups
	600ml (1 pint)	2$^1/_2$ cups	2$^1/_2$ cups
Cup measures (solid)	500g (1 lb) butter	2 cups	2 cups
	200g (7oz) long-grain rice	1 cup	1 cup
	500g (1 lb) sugar	2 cups	2 cups
	50g (2oz) chopped onion	$^1/_2$ cup	$^1/_2$ cup
	50g (2oz) soft breadcrumbs	1 cup	1 cup
	125g (4oz) dry breadcrumbs	1 cup	1 cup
	500g (1 lb) plain flour	4 cups	4 cups
	50g (2oz) thinly sliced mushrooms	$^1/_2$ cup	$^1/_2$ cup
	125g (4oz) grated Cheddar cheese (lightly packed)	1 cup	1 cup
	125g (4oz) chopped nuts	1 cup	1 cup

*British standard tablespoon =15ml; American standard tablespoon = 14.2ml;
Australian standard tablespoon = 20ml.
(**Note**: Due to the nature of most of the recipes in this book, differences between tablespoon capacities should not have any adverse effect on the taste of the food.)

+American measuring cup = 250ml (8fl oz); Australian measuring cup = 250ml (8fl oz).
 (**Note**: British pint = 20floz; American pint = 16floz; Australian pint = 20floz)

Index

Acknowledgements

I would like to take this opportunity to express my sincere thanks to Sarah Lavelle, my editor, for her extremely helpful, creative and thoughtful advice on the 're-vamping' of The Barbecue Book. Thanks also to Nick Bartolucci for his splendid work on the design front. I am also greatly indebted to talented Myles New for the fresh and modern touch he brought to the food photography and to Marina Filippelli for her invaluable contribution to the food 'choreography'.

I would also like to take the opportunity to reiterate my thanks, expressed on other occasions, to my readers and countless millions of barbecue aficionados throughout the world, for their sterling support of farmers, butchers, fishermen, fishmongers, breweries, wine producers, vegetable and fruit growers, oil producers, sauce manufacturers, etc. ... not forgetting makers of barbecues, barbecue accessories and fuel.